BRITAIN AND EUROPE SINCE 1945

Britain and Europe since 1945

ALEX MAY

LONGMAN
LONDON AND NEW YORK

Addison Wesley Longman Limited,
Edinburgh Gate,
Harlow,
Essex CM20 2JE,
United Kingdom
and Associated Companies throughout the world.

*Published in the United States of America
by Addison Wesley Longman Inc. New York*

First published 1999

ISBN 0 582 30778 3 PPR

Visit Addison Wesley Longman on the world wide web at http://www.awl-he.com

British Library Cataloguing-in-Publication Data

A catalogue record for this book is available from the British Library

Library of Congress Cataloging-in-Publication Data

May, Alex (Alex Charles)
      Britain and Europe since 1945 / Alex May.
         p.   cm. (Seminar studies in history)
      Includes bibliographical references (p.) and
   index.
      ISBN 0-582-30778-3
      1. Europe—Relations—Great Britain. 2. Great
   Britain—Relations—Europe. 3. Great Britain-
   -Politics and government—1945- I. Title
   II. Series.
   D1065. G7M375 1999
   303.48'24104—dc21

                                                    98-28607
                                                         CIP

Set by 7 in 10/12 Sabon
Printed in Malaysia , LSP

CONTENTS

AN INTRODUCTION TO THE SERIES

Such is the pace of historical enquiry in the modern world that there is an ever-widening gap between the specialist article or monograph, incorporating the results of current research, and general surveys, which inevitably become out of date. Seminar Studies in History are designed to bridge this gap. The series was founded by Patrick Richardson in 1966 and his aim was to cover major themes in British, European and World history. Between 1980 and 1996 Roger Lockyer continued his work, before handing the editorship over to Clive Emsley and Gordon Martel. Clive Emsley is Professor of History at the Open University, while Gordon Martel is Professor of International History at the University of Northern British Columbia, Canada and Senior Research Fellow at De Montfort University.

All the books are written by experts in their field who are not only familiar with the latest research but have often contributed to it. They are frequently revised, in order to take account of new information and interpretations. They provide a selection of documents to illustrate major themes and provoke discussion, and also a guide to further reading. The aim of *Seminar Studies* is to clarify complex issues without over-simplifying them, and to stimulate readers into deepening their knowledge and understanding of major themes and topics.

NOTE ON REFERENCING SYSTEM

Readers should note that numbers in square brackets [5] refer them to the corresponding entry in the Bibliography at the end of the book (specific page numbers are given in italics). A number in square brackets preceded by *Doc.* [*Doc. 5*] refers readers to the corresponding item in the Documents section which follows the main text.

ACKNOWLEDGEMENTS

The publishers would like to thank the following for permission to reproduce copyright material: Macmillan Ltd for two tables from *British Political Facts, 1900–94* by David and Gareth Butler, 1994; Sir Colin Marshall for a letter from the *Financial Times*, 11 March 1997; Sir Teddy Taylor for a letter from *The Times*, 11 February 1997; Financial Times Professional Ltd for extracts from *From the Six to the Twelve: The Enlargement of the European Communities*, by Frances Nicholson and Roger East, published by Longman Group UK Limited in 1987; ©The Economist, London for an extract from 10 July 1950; Her Majesty's Stationery Office for Documents on British Policy Overseas Series I Vol V, Series II Vol I, Series II Vol III; Various PRO documents PRO FCAB 128/48 c(51)32), PRO CAB 128/29 cm(55)19), PRO T234/203), PRO CAB 134/1820, EQ (60)27); Cmnd 1565 and Cmnd 4715; *Britain's New Deal in Europe*, published in May 1975; Crown Copyright is reproduced with the permission of the Controller of Her Majesty's Stationery Office.

Whilst every effort has been made to trace the owners of copyright material, in a few cases this has proved to be problematic and we take this opportunity to offer our apologies to any copyright holders whose rights we may have unwittingly infringed.

PART ONE: THE BACKGROUND

1 BRITAIN AND EUROPE BEFORE 1945

'I am here in a country which hardly resembles the rest of Europe', the French philosopher Montesquieu declared during a visit to Britain in 1729. A number of historians have confirmed the substance of his observation. Indeed, Alan Macfarlane has argued that as early as the fifteenth century the decline of serfdom, the rise of a market economy and the existence of a distinctive legal system had produced in England (although not necessarily in Wales, Scotland or Ireland) 'a society in which almost every aspect of the culture was diametrically opposed to that of the surrounding nations' [56 p. 165]. While such arguments should not be pressed too far, most historians would agree that the developments of the sixteenth to nineteenth centuries reinforced rather than diminished whatever elements of separateness and distinctness existed. The religious Reformation, although paralleled by developments on the continent, was unique both in its origins and its consequences, and provided the English and lowland Scots with a peculiar sense of providential destiny. The political changes of the mid-seventeenth to early eighteenth centuries – the Civil War of 1642–60, the 'Glorious' Revolution of 1688 and the Act of Union of 1707 – reinforced this sense of uniqueness. The integration of Britain itself was accompanied by a new and assertive role as a maritime power and by the steady accumulation of a vast overseas empire. War, religion, empire, prosperity and parliamentary 'freedom' combined to forge a widespread and active 'British' patriotism, which defined itself largely by opposition to the culture of continental Europe. The industrial revolution, which transformed the British economy earlier and more thoroughly than any of its continental neighbours, gave added impetus to the 'public myth of uniqueness' which had already taken hold [47 p. 149, 52].

The nineteenth century was Britain's heyday, the period of its greatest relative economic and political power. The British Empire encompassed a quarter of the earth's land surface and a similar proportion of its inhabitants. It was perhaps inevitable that the British should see themselves not only as unique amongst Europeans, but also as separate and different; and that British policy towards the continent should be characterised (in Lord Salisbury's famous words) by 'splendid isolation'. Yet even at this high point many recognised that Britain was still a part of Europe; that British culture and British power were reflections of more general European trends. Towards the end of the century, the differences between Britain and its continental neighbours palpably diminished. Other countries industrialised – some more proficiently than Britain. The Scandinavian countries, Belgium, the Netherlands and France (after 1870) maintained political systems at least as 'liberal' and democratic as Britain's. Moreover, centuries of history confirmed that Britain could hardly remain indifferent to developments across the Channel. By the close of the century the dangers of isolation were becoming apparent. Europe was increasingly dominated by a powerful and expansionist Germany, which now embarked on an ambitious naval programme. Colonial conflict was becoming ever more likely. The South African war of 1899–1902 administered a sharp shock to the British psyche: the whole of Europe was hostile, while all available British forces were tied up by a handful of Dutch settlers. As the new century dawned, British politicians scrambled to shore up the 'balance of power', and with it Britain's position. Alliances were concluded with Japan in 1902, with France in 1904, and with Russia in 1907. By these alliances, however, Britain merely increased the tensions in Europe, which was now firmly divided into two armed camps. When war finally came in 1914, it was almost a relief [15, 55].

BRITAIN AND EUROPE BETWEEN THE WARS

The First World War was unlike any previous war and very different from the war which had been expected. It lasted more than four years, cost upwards of 20 million lives, and resulted in the devastation of large parts of Europe. Three empires were dismembered (the German, the Austro-Hungarian and the Ottoman), and a fourth (the Russian) collapsed. Britain and France emerged victorious only through the mobilisation of their extensive imperial resources and the intervention of the United States. President Wilson demanded a generous peace. Britain, and even more, France, demanded retribution. The resultant Treaty of Versailles was a dangerous mismatch of idealism and vindictiveness. Germany lost large chunks of primarily German-speaking territory, was forced to pledge vast sums in reparations (most of which were never paid) and suffered the indignity of numerous restrictions on its national sovereignty – hardly the most favourable conditions in which to embark upon the experiment of democracy. Meanwhile, peace was entrusted to the twin principles of national self-determination (which resulted in the 'Balkanisation' of central and eastern Europe) and collective security, the latter to operate through a League of Nations dependent on consensus and the voluntary co-ordination of national policies. At one stage, Britain promised to guarantee France's security – but only on condition that the United States did so too. America's withdrawal from the agreement, from the League of Nations, and indeed from any entanglement in the affairs of continental Europe, nullified the proposal. Without such support, Britain was still far from ready to make an irreversible 'continental commitment' [55].

One of the major effects of the war was to increase Britain's preoccupation with the empire and Commonwealth. On the one hand, the empire experienced one last burst of expansion, with the acquisition of 'mandated' territories in the Pacific, Africa and the Middle East. On the other, a series of crises in India, Egypt and Ireland diverted resources and absorbed government and public attention. Some historians have argued that the interwar years illustrated the steady decline of British imperial power. Others have argued that, strategically and politically, the empire was more important to Britain than ever [53, 54]. In economic terms, this was certainly true. Between 1910 and 1914, the empire accounted for 25 per cent of Britain's imports and 36 per cent of its exports; by 1930–34 the figures had increased to 31 and 42 per cent and by 1935–39 to 39.5 and 49 per cent. British overseas investment also increasingly followed the flag, 46 per cent going to the empire in 1911–13 and 59 per cent in 1927–29 [13 *p. 261*].

Moreover, the war accelerated the evolution of the self-governing 'Dominions' (Canada, Australia, New Zealand and South Africa) into semi-independent states, as recognised by their separate representation in the League of Nations and by the Statute of Westminster in 1931. The altered status of the Dominions made it more important for Britain to frame its foreign policy with one eye on its imperial partners, if the unity of the empire were to be maintained. This effectively limited Britain's ability to play a major role in Europe. A succession of incidents in the early 1920s revealed the potential for friction and disunity. In 1922 Canada and South Africa refused to support British intervention at Chanak, designed to prevent Turkey from re-establishing a foothold in Europe. In 1924 Canada again led the way, by refusing to ratify the Treaty of Lausanne, on the grounds that it had not been represented at the negotiations. In 1925 it was the British government which broke ranks, agreeing by the Treaty of Locarno to guarantee the borders between France, Belgium, the Netherlands and Germany, without any similar commitment on the part of the Dominions. Locarno caused a major rift in Anglo-Dominion relations, which subsequent British governments were anxious to heal. Significantly, the Foreign Secretary at the time, Austen Chamberlain, defended the Treaty on the grounds that it reduced rather than extended Britain's liabilities in Europe [15 *p. 106, 55*].

Britain stood aloof from all the major developments in the pre-history of European integration in these years. A British branch of the Pan-Europa movement was established, but it was dominated by imperialists such as Leo Amery, who saw European unity (without Britain) as the natural counterpart to closer union of the empire. British industry remained outside the negotiations which led to the formation of transnational cartels in steel and other industries in the late 1920s. When the French Foreign Minister, Aristide Briand, proposed European economic integration leading to 'some kind of federal bond' [49 *p. 220*], in 1929, it was partly the British reaction (although, much more, the world economic depression following the Wall Street crash and the breakdown of democracy in Germany) which ensured that the proposal led nowhere [59]. The main effect of the Briand plan in Britain was to strengthen the hand of those who favoured economic integration of the empire. 'If we do not think imperially, we shall have to think continentally', was Neville Chamberlain's, as he saw it sombre, warning in 1929 [50 *p. 79, 49*]. The economic depression of the 1930s led to the abandonment of free trade with Europe in favour of an imperial economic bloc. Robert Boyce has seen this period as the first of a series of 'missed opportunities' for Britain in Europe. Had British ministers proposed an 'open-ended, non-federal, liberal approach to the re-establishment of a European-wide market' instead of turning to the empire, they would have met with a widespread favourable response from other European countries [51 *p. 31*]. Be that as it may, British priorities were clear.

It was in these circumstances that the British policy of limited commitment to Europe took the form of 'appeasement', i.e. the policy of attempting to placate Germany by acquiescing in its overturning of the Versailles settlement. The origins of this policy can be traced back even to before the signing of the Versailles Treaty, when Lloyd George, largely unsuccessfully, tried to soften the terms to be imposed on Germany. It acquired greater force as a result of the Ruhr crisis of

1922–23, when French and Belgian troops occupied Germany, precipitating the near-collapse of the German economy and the first major crisis of German democracy. Successive British governments launched initiatives designed to produce a peaceful revision of the Versailles terms. It was not, therefore, a new policy which the Macdonald, Baldwin and Chamberlain governments adopted after Hitler came to power in 1933. What condemned their policy was the naivety and vigour with which they pursued it. Yet the pressures leading to such a policy were intense. The Dominions, by and large, opposed any commitment to Europe. The United States had retreated into its isolationist shell, cursing the 'old' world indiscriminately. Britain itself was overstretched. The British public was still wedded to support of the League of Nations. Finally, until his invasion of the rump Czech state in March 1939, Hitler was careful to portray his actions as merely pursuing the principle of national self-determination. Britain's abandonment of 'appeasement' came too late to retrieve the situation. Between March and August 1939 Britain and France made last-minute commitments to the remaining central and eastern European states. These did not prevent Hitler from invading Poland on 1 September 1939. Two days later, Britain was at war [12, 55].

THE SECOND WORLD WAR

The last year of peace and the first year of war witnessed a remarkable growth of pro-European federalist ideas and activities in Britain, sponsored in particular by the Federal Union movement [48, 57]. The latter, launched in July 1939, reached a peak of 12,000 active members organised into 300 branches, by May 1940. At one point the leader of the Labour Party, Clement Attlee, gave his support, declaring that 'Europe must federate or perish' [48 *p. 118*]. The Foreign Office was initially sceptical. Nevertheless, the government appreciated the propaganda value of European federalist ideas. Various proposals were discussed but these were soon narrowed down to the central concept of Anglo-French union. Even as Hitler was unleashing his devastating *blitzkrieg* against France, Jean Monnet and Sir Arthur Salter were entrusted with drafting a declaration of 'indissoluble' economic and political union. The British Cabinet approved the text on the afternoon of 16 June 1940 and immediately transmitted it to the French government at Bordeaux [*Doc. 1*]. The French Prime Minister, Paul Reynaud, was 'transfigured with joy'; but the majority of his colleagues argued that the proposal could do little to help a France now defeated and overrun by German forces. Reynaud resigned, and his successor General Pétain initiated the negotiations which left half of France under German occupation and the other half under the control of the Vichy regime. General de Gaulle – at that stage a mere Under-Secretary in the War Department – declared his intention to continue the war as leader of the 'Free French', but it was clear that without British support he amounted to little [30].

The events of May and June 1940 marked both the high point of support for European federation in Britain and the beginning of its effective demise. The Federal Union's membership dropped below 2,000 by the end of 1940. Its ideas subsequently enjoyed a new lease of life on the continent, providing inspiration to the anti-fascist resistance, which (especially in France and Italy) became firmly committed to a federal reconstruction of Europe. Many of the governments-in-exile which gathered in London during the war also became fervent advocates of a federal solution. In Britain itself, however, the idea of European federation receded into the distant background [48, 57].

Britain's wartime experience was very different from that of the other European countries which would later form the European Union.* After the fall of France, Britain and its empire 'stood alone'. Britain's retreat from Europe, at Dunkirk, was turned into a national victory. Its national institutions stood the test and its sense of national identity and pride emerged strengthened by the war. There was no crisis of the nation-state, as there was in Germany and Italy, and in the countries which they conquered. Moreover, the globalisation of the war served to emphasise the importance of Britain's extra-European links. Europe was but one of two major, and innumerable minor, theatres of war. The empire and Commonwealth were crucial to Britain's survival. But it was only with the help of the Soviet Union and the United States that Britain was able to turn survival into victory. The fact that Britain was the weakest of the 'Big Three' merely underlined the importance of maintaining good relations with the emerging 'superpowers'.

British postwar planning did not really get under way until 1944–45 and then it was largely predicated on the hope of continued co-operation with both Russia and the United States. It was accepted that a strong France was now a major British interest, and the British government fought successfully for French representation in the United Nations Security Council, and for a French occupation zone in Germany. Nevertheless, the building of a closer relationship was complicated by Britain's own financial and economic weakness, by differences over Germany (which France wanted dismembered) and the Middle East (where France was attempting to re-establish its empire), and by the general difficulty of doing business with de Gaulle. The latter's demands for recognition of French 'grandeur', personified by himself, caused Churchill on several occasions to regret the way he had built de Gaulle up. De Gaulle in turn never forgave Churchill (or indeed Britain) for his candid assertion that in the event of any quarrel between France and the United States, Britain 'would almost certainly side with' the United States [30 *p. 56*].

As the war in Europe drew to a close, the idea of British leadership of a more integrated western Europe again gathered support in Foreign Office circles. In an influential memorandum on 'Stocktaking after VE-Day', Sir Orme Sargent argued that only by leadership of western Europe as well as the Commonwealth could Britain continue to rank as one of the 'Big Three' [46, 58, 60]. Nevertheless, Britain's main preoccupations lay elsewhere: with co-operation (rather than competition) with the United States and Russia; with consolidating the wartime unity of the empire and Commonwealth; and with the rebuilding of Britain itself. From being the world's greatest creditor nation in 1939, Britain had become the world's greatest debtor. Moreover, as a result of the war Britain had lost most of its overseas markets and was expected to run a balance of trade deficit of some £2 billion a year when American Lend-Lease (effectively a form of aid) came to an end, as it did abruptly, in August 1945. Britain would have to increase its production and exports dramatically if it were merely to maintain prewar standards of living. This was without any of the schemes for a welfare state which, by 1945, figured largely in the postwar planning of all the major political parties.

PART TWO: BRITAIN AND EUROPE SINCE 1945

2 LABOUR'S EUROPE, 1945–51

Domestic considerations were uppermost in British electors' minds when they voted on 5 July 1945 to elect a Labour government with a Commons majority of 146. The new Prime Minister, Clement Attlee, was a good party manager but hardly a forceful or charismatic personality. The same could not be said of Ernest Bevin, Foreign Secretary until ill-health forced his retirement on 9 March 1951 (when Herbert Morrison replaced him). Unusually for a twentieth-century British government, the conduct of British foreign policy was firmly in the hands of the foreign secretary rather than the prime minister of the day. A former leader of Britain's largest trade union, the TGWU, and the dominant figure on the Labour right, Bevin was memorably described by Churchill as a 'working-class John Bull' [64, 78].

The hallmark of Bevin's foreign policy was Atlanticism – the pursuit of close co-operation with the United States. For that reason, he was often criticised by the left wing of his party, who favoured a more robustly 'socialist' foreign policy. A frequent charge was that Bevin had been 'nobbled' by the Foreign Office [76]. Later commentators gave the charge a different twist. In their view, Bevin and his successor Morrison were deluded by the Foreign Office, by Atlanticism and by a kind of *folie de grandeur* into being 'anti-European'. Thus the scene was set for a series of 'missed opportunities' for Britain to take the lead in European integration [28, 43, 81].

Recent historians, with the benefit of access to private and Cabinet papers and Foreign Office files, have modified this picture to a large extent. Bevin did share a number of ideas and assumptions with his Foreign Office advisers, but these were by no means as 'anti-European' as has often been assumed [62, 78]. As early as 1927, he had advocated the creation of a European common market [50]. Almost his first act on entering the Foreign Office in 1945 was to call a meeting of his senior officials at which he outlined a 'grand design' for western European co-operation, based on a close relationship between Britain and France [*Doc. 2a*]. His approach differed fundamentally from that adopted by 'the Six'* (i.e. the six original members of the European Communities*) after 1950, in that he favoured 'practical programmes' rather than 'ambitious schemes'. For him, any real progress would have to be gradual, and based on the principle of intergovernmentalism (i.e., the voluntary co-ordination of national policies) rather than supranationalism (the building of new institutions at a level above the nation-state). Nevertheless, Bevin succeeded in effecting almost a revolution in British foreign policy, by committing Britain to economic, political and military co-operation with western Europe to an unprecedented peacetime degree [38, 82, 84].

THE INTERNATIONAL CONTEXT

At the Conservative Party conference in October 1948, Churchill observed that there were 'three great circles among the free nations and democracies': the British Empire, the 'English Speaking World', and 'United Europe'. 'You will see that we are the only country which has a great part in every one of them. We stand, in fact, at the very point of junction.' This idea immediately struck a chord with contemporaries. Anthony Eden spoke of 'three unities'; later, a 'three-legged stool' [66 *pp. 155–6*]. Similarly, Bevin described 'three main pillars of our policy, the Commonwealth in some degree, Western Europe and the United States' [2 *p. 261*]. It is tempting to ask which of the 'circles' was most important to Britain. But, as Oliver Franks (Ambassador to Washington, and one of Bevin's key advisers) later made clear, each was important in its own way.

> If you are thinking in strategic and military terms there is no question that our relationship with the United States was the priority. On the other hand, in terms of tradition, emotion and affection, the Commonwealth came first; and in terms of our neighbours without whom we were literally not safe or secure, then Europe came very much into the picture. [34 *p. 58*]

British policy-makers firmly believed that the three 'circles' were not incompatible. It was not so much a question of prioritising as of balancing Britain's commitments to all three.

With hindsight, the years 1945–51 marked a radical change in Britain's relationship with the empire/Commonwealth. The independence of India and Pakistan in 1947 was by far the most significant step in the process of decolonisation which, over the next twenty years, was to divest Britain of most (but not all) of its empire. Some writers have argued that Britain should have seen the writing on the wall and committed itself then to a European future [43]. At the time, however, the implications of independence were not at all clear. The 'old' Dominions had effectively been independent for many years, but over that period their value to Britain had, if anything, increased. Similarly, the Indian subcontinent was expected to remain firmly within a British sphere of influence. Moreover, decolonisation was accompanied, at least initially, by a determination to consolidate and concentrate on what remained of the empire. In Africa, in particular, the Second World War was followed by a revival of imperialism, facilitated by unprecedented levels of funding for colonial development [11, 54]. In more general terms, the empire/Commonwealth remained crucial to Britain's economic position. As late as 1950, the Commonwealth accounted for nearly 50 per cent of British exports, Europe for little more than 25 per cent. Britain's major economic problem was the so-called 'sterling-dollar gap': the difficulty of earning enough dollars by exports to pay for dollar imports. The empire/Commonwealth formed the core of the 'sterling bloc' (the group of countries using sterling as their trading currency), which was the key to Britain's success in resolving this problem. As Scott Newton has observed, Britain's economic vulnerability 'stimulated not a steady retreat from empire but a new spasm of imperialism' [77 *p. 178*].

Although the Second World War witnessed the rise of the 'special relationship' between Britain and the United States, tensions between the two were present even during the war. America saved Britain from bankruptcy in 1940–41, but cancelled the Lend-Lease programme as soon as the war ended, and rapidly dismantled most of the joint decision-making structures which had ensured their close collaboration throughout the war. The Americans resented that any assistance they provided might be used to prop up the British Empire; they disliked the sterling bloc, imperial preference and any other obstacle to free trade. The British, fearing that America would revert to isolationism (as had been the case after 1919), saw the special relationship as a complicating factor in their relations with Europe: the Americans, they initially assumed, would object to the creation of anything that resembled a regional trading bloc. After about 1947, America began to press in the opposite direction, in favour of the integration of Europe (including Britain), with an urgency and a predilection for the American federal model which frequently irritated Britain. For two decades following the Second World War Britain tried to balance the attractions of Europe against America and had to deal with the resentment and opposition of both [42, 68].

The dominating fact of the period 1945-51 was the breakdown of 'Big Three' co-operation and the emergence of the 'Cold War' between Russia and the West. Tensions had already been apparent during wartime, and by March 1946 (the time of his famous 'iron curtain' speech) Churchill was convinced that the breakdown was permanent. The Labour government initially distanced itself from Churchill's views. Nevertheless, a series of incidents – from the breakdown of the Moscow and London conferences in April and December 1947, through the Prague coup of February 1948, to the Berlin blockade of June 1948 to May 1949 – confirmed the mutual hostility of the Soviet and Western camps. Some commentators have argued that Britain was dragged into the Cold War by its dependence on the United States but recent historians have emphasised the extent to which Britain took a leading role in attempting to influence American policy. The 'Truman doctrine' of March 1947 (committing the United States to the 'containment' of communism) was a direct response to Britain's decision to pull out of Greece, while Bevin played a key role in organising the European response to the Marshall Plan and in the creation of NATO, both of which exacerbated East-West divisions [42, 68, 80]. Inevitably, the Cold War altered the parameters of Britain's relationships with all three 'circles' and determined the framework of subsequent British policy.

BEVIN, EUROPE AND 'WESTERN UNION'

Bevin's 'grand design' of August 1945 envisaged the progressive enlargement of economic and political co-operation with the maritime 'fringes' of Europe, starting with France [*Doc. 2a*]. A number of historians have argued that the gradual integration of western Europe, through intergovernmental rather than supranational institutions, represented the consistent aim of his foreign policy until at least 1949 [38, 65, 84]. Indeed, Bevin was even briefly attracted to the idea of western Europe and the Commonwealth constituting a 'third force' – 'a stable group between the United States and Soviet Russia', as he put it in October 1947 [82 *p.* 66]. Britain's expectation of leadership of such a group was clear. Britain's 'primary objective', a Foreign Office official noted in December 1946, was 'by close association with our neighbours to create a European group which will enable us to deal on a footing of equality with our two gigantic colleagues, the USA and the USSR' [80 *p. 435*].

Little came of the 'third force' idea, or even of the more limited idea of British involvement in western European co-operation, in the years 1945–46, for a number of reasons. Britain's relations with France remained difficult even after de Gaulle's resignation in January 1946. The future of Germany was a particular sticking-point. The strength of communism in France and the chronic instability of French politics were others. More generally, there was a lack of British confidence in western Europe's economic prospects. Britain's was by far the strongest economy in western Europe, outproducing France and Germany combined. The Treasury and the Board of Trade consistently argued that Britain had little to gain, and much to lose, from closer association with Europe. Finally, the international context, which in 1945–46 was still dominated by hopes of a 'Big Three' partnership, put a severe restraint on any moves towards the creation of a European 'bloc' [38, 62].

The deterioration of the international situation, accompanied by a thaw in Anglo-French relations, led to a revival of Bevin's interest in western European integration, in the years 1947–48. Again, there were echoes of the 'third force' idea, and Bevin clearly envisaged wide-ranging economic as well as military co-operation, including a customs union. The most forceful exposition of Bevin's ideas was in his speech to the House of Commons in January 1948. 'Britain cannot stand outside of Europe', he declared. It was time to think of western Europe 'as a unit'. The British government 'should do all we can to foster both the spirit and the machinery of co-operation', which should be underpinned by collaboration in the development of western Europe's 'overseas territories' [*Doc. 2b*, 70].

Again, few concrete measures emanated from Bevin's enthusiasm. The Treasury and Colonial Office opposed his ideas for developing the colonial empires. Bevin himself became sidetracked into concentrating on military rather than economic integration. The continued deterioration of Soviet-western relations, and signs that America might now be induced to commit itself to the defence of western Europe, encouraged him to make Anglo-American co-operation his priority. Finally, differences of approach between Britain and the continental countries (especially France) forced Britain onto the defensive [62, 82]. By October 1949, Bevin and the Chancellor, Sir Stafford Cripps, were arguing that the government should 'not ... involve themselves in the economic affairs of Europe beyond the point from which they could, if they wished, withdraw': 'we must remain, as we have always been in the past, different in character from other European nations and fundamentally incapable of wholehearted integration with them' [64 *p. 734*].

THE MARSHALL PLAN AND THE OEEC

In contrast to Europe, America looked likely to become a victim of its own economic success in the late 1940s. America's economy had expanded enormously during the war, and by 1947 was exporting $16 billion of goods and importing only $8 billion. Humanitarianism was the dominant theme in the presentation of the American policy of aid to Europe, which became known as the Marshall Plan – but, as a number of historians have pointed out, this was a case in which morality and self-interest happily coincided. Had America not undertaken such a programme, there would undoubtedly have been a balance of payments crisis, leading to a recession in America's export industries and a possible end to American hopes for a multilateral world trade system. Moreover, American policy-makers were now keen to counteract the lure of communism and to re-establish free market capitalism. As Michael Hogan puts it, Marshall aid was conceived in the spirit of 'remaking the Old World in the image of the New' [69, 72 *p. 18*].

Secretary of State George Marshall's offer to provide American aid for a European recovery plan was made in a speech of 5 June 1947. 'The initiative', he emphasised, 'must come from Europe' [64 *p. 404*]. Bevin immediately 'grabbed' the opportunity 'with both hands', as he later told the Commons. In talks with his French counterpart, Georges Bidault, he agreed a framework for devising a common plan. At Bidault's insistence, he endured a highly unsuccessful meeting with the Russian Foreign Minister, Molotov. It was largely Bevin's determination which ensured the creation of the Committee of European Economic Co-operation (CEEC), which co-ordinated the national recovery plans of sixteen western European states, and presented them to Washington as a single programme. Bevin's biographer has described his role in the Marshall Plan negotiations as 'his most decisive personal contribution as Foreign Secretary' [64 *p. 404*]. The CEEC initially requested $28 billion over four years but this was reduced to $19 billion. By the time the Plan came to an end, in 1951, America had in fact donated some $13 billion, of which some $2.7 billion went to Britain [79].

Although other factors were important, the Marshall Plan was undoubtedly the major factor in kick-starting the European economy which, despite setbacks, enjoyed an era of unprecedented prosperity in the 1950s and 1960s. Moreover, the Organisation for European Economic Co-operation* (OEEC) (which replaced the CEEC in April 1948) gave rise to a number of important initiatives, including the European Payments Union of September 1950 and the International

Customs Union Study Group. The latter, established on Bevin's initiative in September 1947, produced many of the ideas which later found expression in the European Communities [75]. Nevertheless, the Marshall Plan and the OEEC were also a source of great difficulty for Britain. Underlying Marshall's offer was an idea common to most American policy-makers, that Europe's problems could in large part be ascribed to the lack of European unity [72]. Bevin was successful in ensuring that the OEEC was intergovernmental rather than supranational in character. Nevertheless, American pressure on Britain to take the lead in integrating Europe was at times intense [38, 82]. The OEEC survived until 1961, when it was replaced by the Organisation for Economic Co-operation and Development (OECD)*. During the 1950s it enjoyed a brief popularity in British governing circles, as an alternative to the more far-reaching proposals emanating from the continent. As a permanent intergovernmental conference, its work was unspectacular but important. In numerous ways it limited the economic sovereignty of Britain and the other member-states.

THE BRUSSELS TREATY AND NATO

British sovereignty was far more severely circumscribed by developments in the defence sphere. In 1945–51, Britain finally accepted a permanent peacetime 'continental commitment' [55]. Initially, Britain was drawn to western Europe by the need to ensure the future containment of Germany rather than of Russia. This ostensibly underlay the Treaty of Dunkirk, signed by Britain and France in March 1947. Kenneth Morgan has argued that Dunkirk was a 'finite, self-contained episode', and was not meant as a step towards European integration [76 *p. 268*]. On the other hand, John Young and Sean Greenwood have argued that it was part of a much broader plan, consistent with Bevin's 'grand design', and with his scheme of 'Western Union' [38, 84]. The Treaty of Brussels, signed by Britain, France and the Benelux* countries in March 1948 gives rise to similar problems of interpretation. Again, Young and Greenwood have emphasised the consistency with Bevin's 'Western Union' speech of January 1948: at the time, Bevin himself said that 'our ultimate aim should be to attain a position in which the countries of Western Europe would be independent both of the US and the Soviet Union' [38 *p. 24*, 84]. Other writers have argued that the Treaty was conceived primarily as a means of persuading the United States that western Europe was doing all it could in its own defence. It was 'a sprat to catch a whale', again in Bevin's own words [64 *p. 537*, 28]. The difficulty of interpretation clearly arises partly from Bevin's own inconsistency; but this in turn reflected the fluidity of strategies and objectives at a time of enormous change.

Only a month after the Brussels Treaty, Bevin and Bidault wrote jointly to Truman that 'we shall require the assistance of the United States in order to organise the effective defence of Western Europe' [78 *p. 134*]. The force of their argument was increased by the Berlin crisis, which precipitated a major war scare. Eventually, in April 1949, the United States, Canada, Denmark, Norway, Iceland, Italy and Portugal joined the Brussels Treaty powers by creating the North Atlantic Treaty Organisation (NATO)* [29, 63]. Sir Nicholas Henderson has described NATO as 'a British invention' [71 *p. 360*]. While this was an exaggeration, Bevin certainly pushed hard for such a Treaty as soon as he realised that 'in the last resort we cannot rely on the European countries' [62 *p. 228*]. NATO confirmed America's commitment to the defence of western Europe, but it also symbolised Britain's preference for 'Atlantic' rather than purely west European solutions to the problem of international organisation.

CHURCHILL AND THE COUNCIL OF EUROPE

Europe was a secondary concern for Churchill during the war and his thoughts on postwar European organisation were extremely vague. It was only after becoming leader of the opposition that he turned his attention to the European scene. He then did so in spectacular fashion. At Zürich in September 1946 he made an impassioned plea for Franco-German reconciliation as the first step towards a 'United States of Europe'. He was careful to describe Britain and the Commonwealth as only 'friends and sponsors' of the new Europe but his caution was often overlooked [*Doc. 3a*]. Churchill's speech galvanised support for integration in Europe, including Britain, where his son-in-law, Duncan Sandys, founded the United Europe Movement. This was one of the prime movers behind the Hague Congress of May 1948, at which Churchill welcomed the Brussels Treaty and the OEEC, but called for 'a parallel policy of political unity', in the form of a Council of Europe. He recognised that this involved 'some sacrifice or merger of national sovereignty. But it is also possible ... to regard it as the gradual assumption by all nations concerned of that larger sovereignty which can also protect their diverse and distinctive customs and characteristics' [92 *p. 407*].

Churchill's activities embarrassed and irritated Bevin, who not unreasonably thought that Churchill was trying to have things both ways – to appear as the champion of Europe, yet to be equally cautious when it came to practical measures [34 *pp*. 56–8]. Unfortunately for Bevin, Churchill's call found a ready response in Europe and at the July 1948 Brussels Treaty meeting France and Belgium put forward a proposal for a European Assembly. Bevin described the proposal as a 'Pandora's Box ... full of Trojan horses' [64 *p*. 659]. Nevertheless, he realised that Europe must have its 'talking shop', and he therefore put forward his own proposals for a more limited, intergovernmental body. The Council of Europe* which finally emerged represented a compromise between French and British views. The Committee of Ministers held most power, but the Assembly (composed of delegations from national parliaments) attracted most attention [78, 84]. Like the OEEC, the Council of Europe has continued to work steadily but unspectacularly, producing conventions and agreements on such subjects as terrorism, human rights and the environment. Since 1959 it has included a European Court of Human Rights,* whose decisions, though not binding, are usually complied with. The Council of Europe is separate from and includes more countries than the European Union, although, confusingly, the European Parliament* used to meet in the Council of Europe building in Strasbourg and the European Union has adopted the Council of Europe's flag.

THE SCHUMAN AND PLEVEN PLANS

That the British government was losing the lead, and indeed was losing interest, in European integration was made clear by the Council of Europe episode. It was confirmed by the British reaction to the Schuman Plan,* which was sprung on an unsuspecting British government on 9 May 1950. On that day the French Foreign Minister, Robert Schuman, announced a proposal to 'pool' French and German coal and steel production under a supranational 'High Authority', as 'the first concrete foundation of a European federation' [22 *p*. 1]. France and Germany were the only countries specifically mentioned in Schuman's proposal but it was made clear that other countries would be welcome to join.

Some writers have seen Schuman's initiative as evidence of a far-sighted French strategy for uniting and bringing peace to Europe. Coal and steel were the basic war industries, and to remove them from national control would be a major step towards removing the possibility of war between participating countries [28, 43]. On the other hand, the work of Alan Milward and others has demonstrated that Schuman was motivated as much by French national interests as by European idealism [75]. The real author of the plan was Jean Monnet. As the head of the French *Commissariat au Plan*, he was acutely aware that France's economic recovery, and also the survival of Bidault's administration, depended on the continued importation of large quantities of cheap German coal. But these supplies were endangered by the boom in the West German economy following the Marshall Plan and the steady removal of Allied restrictions on German economic sovereignty. France was expected to have to make further concessions at the talks on Germany scheduled to start in London on 11 May. Monnet had already tried, unsuccessfully, to secure imports of British coal within the framework of an Anglo-French economic union. He now saw supranational control of French and German coal and steel as the only way to safeguard French recovery. As Milward has observed, 'the Schuman Plan was called into existence to save the Monnet Plan' [75 *p. 475*].

National interests also dictated the responses of other western European countries. Konrad Adenauer, the German Chancellor, leapt at the opportunity to rehabilitate Germany. The smaller countries, Belgium, the Netherlands and Luxembourg, while in some cases dubious about the supranational principle, recognised that they could not afford to be shut out of the French and German markets. Italy, like Germany, hoped for rehabilitation, but also for help in expanding its relatively minor industrial base. Significantly, the three leading politicians, Schuman, Adenauer and the Italian Alcide de Gasperi, were all from border areas, and therefore acutely aware of the interdependence of western Europe.

Bevin's initial reaction to the Schuman Plan was one of pique. Both Adenauer and Acheson (the American Secretary of State, who was in London at the time the plan was announced) had been forewarned, whereas he had not. This was despite an agreement between Britain, France and America not to publicise any proposals concerning Germany without prior negotiation between the three. The suspicion that Schuman did not really want Britain's participation was increased by his insistence that negotiations should focus on the form a supranational authority should take, not on the principle of supranationality itself. Finally, the British were presented with a 24-hour ultimatum, on 1 June 1950, at a time when the three leading Cabinet figures, Attlee, Bevin and Cripps, were either on holiday or in hospital.

It is tempting to emphasise the role of personality and circumstance in the British decision not to take part in the Schuman negotiations but it is clear that there were substantial reasons for British non-involvement. In the first place, the European economies were still devastated by the war. In coal and steel, Britain was more or less self-sufficient and exported very little to Europe. On the other hand, Britain's exports to its major markets, the Commonwealth and sterling bloc, were likely to suffer if Britain associated more closely with Europe. The economic arguments for joining were, therefore, by no means compelling. Secondly, the Labour government had nationalised coal and was committed to the nationalisation of steel, whereas the Schuman Plan appeared to involve the formation of an effective cartel, run in the interests of industrialists. As Herbert Morrison exclaimed, 'the Durham miners won't wear it!' [64 *p. 780*]. Thirdly, the British government had long made clear its preference for intergovernmental rather than supranational forms of integration. In the case of the Schuman Plan, the supranational commitment was dangerously open-ended. Finally, it was by no means clear that the project would succeed. Franco-German hostility was still a potent force, and Schuman's position was by no means secure. It was clearly prudent not to put the government's credibility at risk by supporting a proposal whose survival was so unclear [74, 81].

It would be wrong to portray the government's attitude as consistently or entirely negative. It was recognised that such an attitude would lead Britain to incur the 'utmost political odium' not only from Europe, but also from the United States [74 *p. 124*, 42]. The idea of joining the negotiations in order to wreck or modify the Schuman Plan was rejected out of hand [81]. Moreover, Franco-German reconciliation was a primary British interest [*Doc. 4a*]. The policy adopted by the British government was in fact one of 'benevolent neutrality': remaining outside the negotiations, but intending, if they succeeded, to negotiate a form of association which would safeguard both British and European interests [82 *p. 74*].

Nevertheless, the Labour government came under attack both from Europe and America for appearing to be 'anti-European'. At home, *The Economist* criticised the government for failing the 'test' of European commitment [*Doc. 4b*]. Finally, Churchill and his colleagues seized on Europe as a stick with which to beat the government, deriding Bevin's lack of initiative and arguing that Britain could easily have followed the Dutch example by entering the negotiations with stated reservations [92].

The government failed another 'test' of its European commitment later in 1950 when forced to respond to the French Prime Minister René Pleven's plan for a 'European army'. This idea had already been put forward by Churchill at the Council of Europe. Party politics may therefore have been an element in Bevin's reaction. Initially, however, he thought that the proposal should not be taken 'too seriously' [3 *pp. 230–2*]. The Pleven Plan* was clearly a response to Acheson's call for German rearmament within a unified Atlantic force, and again included a supranational authority as a means of controlling Germany without discriminatory restrictions. Bevin expected Pleven to drop the plan, as it would clearly conflict with the American one. When he did not, Bevin became increasingly hostile. He believed that the plan was an attempt to construct a 'third force' which would inevitably undermine NATO. 'We must nip it in the bud', he declared [*Doc. 5a*]. Bevin's options were limited, however, by the attitude of the American government, which welcomed the Pleven initiative [84, 101].

The perception that Britain was hostile to plans for European integration compelled Bevin's successor, Morrison, to issue a joint statement with Schuman and Acheson, in which he welcomed the Pleven initiative. Morrison's biographers have claimed that, more generally, he 'definitely softened' the government's line on Europe [67 *p. 473*]. On the other hand, Geoffrey Warner has argued that the question of personality was irrelevant. Morrison was equally hostile to British membership of the Schuman or Pleven schemes, but he was operating in a context in which Bevin had made Britain's non-membership accepted, and when Britain could therefore afford to put more emphasis on benevolence [82]. As it was, it was Morrison who (with one eye on the approaching election) almost wrecked the Schuman negotiations by refusing to agree to the removal of controls on German industry until Germany honoured an agreement to export scrap metal to Britain [74 *pp. 145–7*].

3 THE CONSERVATIVES' EUROPE, 1951–57

In the general election held on 23 February 1950, the Labour government was returned with a slender Commons majority of five. It decided to go to the polls again on 25 October 1951. Despite increasing its share of the vote (and winning more votes than the Conservatives) it was defeated. The Conservatives went on to achieve the remarkable feat of increasing their majority in two subsequent elections, in 1955 and in 1959. Only on 15 October 1964 did a Labour victory bring an end to thirteen years of Conservative rule.

CHURCHILL, EDEN AND EUROPE

Expectations of a change in Britain's policy towards Europe were running high when Churchill became Prime Minister in October 1951. Churchill had lent his name to the proposal of Anglo–French union in 1940; he had backed the idea of a 'United States of Europe' at Zürich; he had been prominent in the European Movement and the Council of Europe; and he had been a forceful critic of Labour's anti-Europeanism. Moreover, a more positive European policy was favoured by a small but influential group of 'Tory Strasbourgers', including Duncan Sandys, David Maxwell-Fyfe, Harold Macmillan and Robert Boothby. Hopes for a change in policy were soon disappointed, however. The 'Strasbourgers' were safely insulated from responsibility for European policy and the key post of Foreign Secretary went to Anthony Eden (Churchill's successor as Prime Minister after 6 April 1955).

The 'Strasbourgers' date their 'betrayal' very specifically to 28 November 1951 [87 *p. 83*, 97 *pp. 461–3*]. On that date, Maxwell-Fyfe (Home Secretary in the new government) gave a speech at the Council of Europe, in which he promised that 'no genuine method' of European unity 'shall fail for lack of thorough examination' by Britain [102 *p. 928*]. On the same day, Eden gave a press conference in Rome, in which he made clear that Britain had no intention of joining any organisation which resulted from the Pleven talks. Maxwell-Fyfe felt personally insulted but Churchill backed Eden. In a memorandum for the Cabinet, Churchill emphasised that although he was 'not opposed to a European Federation', he 'never thought that Britain or the British Commonwealth should ... become an integral part' [*Doc. 3b*]. As he later put it, 'I meant it for them, not for us' [91 *p. 77*].

A further incident in March 1952 illustrated the weakness of the 'Strasbourgers'. On that occasion, Macmillan put forward a plan for a series of intergovernmental institutions, to replace the Schuman and Pleven schemes. He was resoundingly defeated and seriously considered resignation [97]. It is tempting to see this episode as evidence of a heroic but one-sided conflict between Europhiles and opponents of the European idea. Nevertheless, there were clear limitations to the 'Strasbourger' commitment to Europe. Macmillan was motivated partly by a desire to bolster British influence: 'it is only by adding the leadership of Europe to our leadership of the Empire', he told Churchill after his 1952 defeat, 'that we can bring to bear ... the influence on world affairs which should be ours' [102 *p. 934*]. Macmillan's plan entirely ignored the preference of 'the Six' for supranational rather than intergovernmental institutions. His colleague Boothby was quite open about wanting the Pleven Plan to fail. Arguably, Eden and Churchill were more realistic and effectively more helpful to European integration in believing that 'the Six' should go ahead and build their own institutions [90, 102].

Fundamentally there was little change in British policy towards Europe. The Conservatives operated with the same assumptions, priorities and constraints as Labour. In particular, it was still believed that Britain was a 'world' power, with greater influence and wider responsibilities than any of the other states of north-west Europe. The Commonwealth and sterling bloc were seen as vital to Britain's position. While Britain favoured Franco–German reconciliation, it was not in Britain's interests to see western Europe divided into two groups, nor for western European integration to endanger the stability of the Atlantic alliance. It was still doubted whether 'Little Europe' would succeed with its 'ambitious' schemes. Finally, the Conservatives were as hostile as Labour to any commitment to supranationality. For Britain to join a 'federal' Europe was 'something which we know, in our bones, we cannot do', Eden asserted, in January 1952 [90].

BRITAIN AND THE ECSC

Contrary to British expectations, the Schuman negotiations were concluded swiftly, and the Treaty of Paris* was signed in April 1951. As a result of last-minute concessions to the Dutch, the European Coal and Steel Community (ECSC)* was as much intergovernmental as supranational in character. A powerful Council of Ministers* operated alongside an Assembly and an independent European Court of Justice.* The driving force of the Community was, however, the supranational High Authority – established, with Monnet as President, in August 1952. The common market in coal came into operation in February 1953, and the common market in steel in May 1953. The Community enjoyed a rapid success. Growth rates in the coal and steel industries of 'the Six' consistently outpaced those of Britain [93].

Sean Greenwood has written that 'the return of the Conservatives to office in 1951 made not a scrap of difference to the British response ... to the Schuman Plan' [38 *p. 40*]. This may seem to overstate the case. Christopher Lord has shown that the Labour government had made no real progress with the 'association' idea before October 1951. According to one official, this policy appeared to be that association 'should mean nothing' [74 *p. 141*]. The Conservatives were at least more constructive in attempting to put flesh on the bones of association. But, judged by their results, it is difficult to dissent from Greenwood's conclusion. An Anglo–ECSC Treaty of Association was eventually signed in December 1954, but this provided only for a Council of Association, exchanges of information, and joint action on pricing and supplies. Pressure from the coal and steel industries, trade unions, the Treasury and the Board of Trade ensured that the proposal to move towards a common market in coal and steel was dropped.

EDC, EPC, WEU

The Conservative government again made few significant changes in British policy towards the Pleven Plan. Soon after taking office Eden made clear, in a letter to Churchill, that he proposed to continue Labour's policy. Britain 'should support the Pleven Plan', but 'I have never thought it possible that we could join'. Britain should prepare 'a more modest scheme' to replace the plan should it collapse; but any such scheme should remain secret, to avoid the charge that Britain had acted to 'kill' the plan [*Doc. 5b*]. Churchill himself quickly lost all enthusiasm for a 'European army'. Indeed, Eden had to work hard to restrain him from criticising the plan, which he had now decided would lead to a 'sludgy amalgam' incapable of contributing to the defence of western Europe [103 *p. 83*].

The governments of 'the Six' eventually signed the Treaty to create a European Defence Community (EDC)* on 27 May 1952. The integration of defence clearly raised the question of political control in a more acute form than did the creation of a coal and steel community, and the EDC Treaty contained provisions for the creation of a European Political Community (EPC).* Quite what this meant was not yet agreed, however. Eden put forward his own proposals (the so-called 'Eden Plan') at the beginning of 1952. These envisaged control of both the ECSC and the EDC being exercised by 'the Six' within the context of the Council of Europe operating on three levels: 'the Six' alone, 'the Six' and their associates, and the full Council. Understandably, Monnet and his fellow enthusiasts suspected an attempt to dilute the principle of supranationality, and the Eden Plan made little headway. Instead, the governments of 'the Six' agreed in September 1952 to entrust the assembly of the ECSC with drawing up a constitution for a political community. This it did six months later [91].

The Eden Plan was unhelpful in the context of European aspirations. In other respects, Eden's policy was more constructive. He recognised early on that Britain's attitude might prove a crucial factor in the debate on the EDC proposal. In the spring of 1952 he urged a string of concessions on the Cabinet. The EDC Treaty of May 1952 was accompanied by an Anglo–EDC Treaty, which committed Britain to a military presence on the continent and to joint training and exchanges of officers. Eden made further concessions in response to delays in the ratification process, including representation in EDC institutions, the commitment of a British division to the 'European army' and a promise on future troop levels. However, shifts in the international context doomed the EDC. The death of Stalin and the end of the Korean war lessened the impetus of the proposal. France's difficulties in Indo-China distracted attention and resources and led to the formation of the nationalist government of Pierre Mendès-France. On 30 August 1954 the French Assembly rejected the EDC Treaty, narrowly but decisively [103]. Churchill was pleased: 'I do not blame the French for rejecting the EDC, only for inventing it', he told Eisenhower [101 *p. 94*].

Eden was more pessimistic. The collapse of the EDC was an outcome he had hoped to avoid. France was now likely to drift into isolation or chauvinism. Germany could not but feel slighted. More worrying still, America had already put Europe on notice that it might have to go through an 'agonising reappraisal' of its commitments if the EDC fell through. It was in these circumstances that Eden secured what John Young has described as a 'major diplomatic triumph' [103 *p. 95*]. This was the agreement reached at the London conference of September 1954 (and embodied in treaty form the following month), whereby the Brussels Treaty was extended to create a Western European Union* including Germany and Italy, as a step towards full membership of NATO. German rearmament and the restoration of full German sovereignty were balanced by a new package of British and American military guarantees. Eden's decision to prepare a 'more modest scheme' had paid dividends, and he basked, briefly, in the reputation of a good European [98, 103].

THE MESSINA CONFERENCE

At the beginning of 1955, Britain's standing in Europe was 'as strong as ever' [105 *p. 199*]. Its attachment to 'practical programmes' rather than 'ambitious schemes' appeared at last to have been vindicated. Within a matter of months, however, the initiative had once more been wrested by 'the Six' and Britain was again reduced to watching from the sidelines. The collapse of the EDC had been a real setback, which threatened the progress and even the viability of the ECSC itself. A '*rélance*' – a re-launch of European integration – was believed by many to be necessary in order to preserve what had already been achieved. Resigning as ECSC President, Monnet launched the 'Action Committee for the United States of Europe', a high-profile pressure group which campaigned for supranational integration in further sectors, notably atomic power. Meanwhile, the Dutch government proposed the creation of a customs union, or 'common market'. These and other proposals were discussed at a meeting of leaders of 'the Six' at Messina, in June 1955. The Messina Conference agreed to further negotiations, under the chairmanship of Paul-Henri Spaak. Britain was invited to send a delegate to the talks. This time, there would be no preconditions [22].

The British government was initially uncertain as to how to respond to this invitation. In Cabinet, Macmillan argued for sending a delegate 'on the same footing as other countries', in order to 'exercise a greater influence on the ... discussions'. The Chancellor, Rab Butler, argued for sending a mere 'observer'. The Cabinet eventually decided to send a 'representative' [*Doc. 6a*]. The man chosen for this job – Russell Bretherton, an official from the Board of Trade – faced a difficult task. Not only did he find himself in the company of far more senior political figures from 'the Six', but he was constantly pressed for an indication of what Britain would find acceptable. This he was unable to give [34 *pp. 178–9*].

The British government's reaction to the Messina invitation was dictated by the inertia of what had by now become established British policy: 'co-operation without commitment', as Bretherton was instructed by London. The opportunity to re-assess British policy was used merely to confirm the assumptions behind this policy. Various committees studied the economic and political aspects of the problem and concluded that Britain could not afford to become an integral part of the new Europe. In economic terms, British participation in the schemes discussed by the Spaak committee would have serious consequences for British industry and agriculture and for the sterling bloc. In political terms, participation might disrupt the Commonwealth and (in the long term) the Anglo–American relationship, and would involve the 'risk that ... we might be taken further along the road of ... political federation than we would wish' [105 *p. 211*].

Bretherton's position, which had always been difficult, quickly became untenable. The longer he remained, the more difficult it would be 'to avoid the presumption that we are committed to the result' [105 *p. 206*]. An appeal by 'the Six' for Britain to send a Cabinet minister to a meeting to discuss progress in September 1955 fell on deaf ears. 'The Six' agreed to restructure the negotiations, with a more powerful central committee charged with formulating actual proposals. Bretherton was instructed to return to Brussels, but to deliver a statement making clear that the British government could not contemplate participating in any new institutions. Moreover, he now put forward British proposals to discuss many of the topics within the looser framework of the Organisation for European Economic Co-operation (OEEC).* Spaak was furious. He made clear that the final report could only be drawn up by the representatives of the six governments who were committed to participation. Bretherton left the committee and did not return. Spaak ever after believed that Britain had withdrawn from the talks. Bretherton, on the other hand, was quite clear that Britain had been 'thrown out' [34, 105].

MISSED OPPORTUNITIES?

The misunderstanding surrounding Bretherton's withdrawal or exclusion was symptomatic of a more deep-rooted failure of communication which plagued relations between Britain and its continental partners throughout the period 1945–57. This in turn reflected a fundamental difference of approach. The British government was willing to talk about practical schemes but only so long as it was understood that it reserved the right to take final decisions later. The continentals, on the other hand, wanted commitment first; the details could be discussed later. Bretherton himself was convinced that the British government had passed up a wonderful opportunity to determine the shape of the new Europe: 'if we had been able to say ... that we accepted "in principle" ... we could have got whatever kind of Common Market* we wanted. I have no doubt of that at all' [34 *p. 179*].

A number of writers have seen Messina as but one – albeit the most striking – of a series of 'missed opportunities' for Britain in Europe. According to this view, the ultimate price Britain paid for such missed opportunities was that it was forced to seek entry to the European Communities at a later date, when institutions and policies had been adopted which were less in tune with, and in some cases inimical to, British views and interests. Monnet believed that the fundamental reason for Britain's wrong-footed diplomacy was a gross miscalculation of its influence in the world. Britain paid 'the price of victory – the illusion that you could maintain what you had, without change' [34 *p. 307*, 43, 108].

One problem with such interpretations is that it is by no means clear which of Britain's 'missed opportunities' was the crucial one. Michael Charlton and Christopher Lord have argued that Britain's abstention from the Schuman Plan and ECSC represented the 'turning-point'. As Lord has pointed out, the ECSC was 'the first of the European Economic Communities that would eventually evolve into the modern European Union'. 'The Six' evolved habits of co-operation which translated relatively easily into further integration. Britain developed an array of arguments against participation which made involvement in future schemes more difficult [74 *p. 2*]. This interpretation is given weight by the fact that Britain's reaction to the Messina negotiations was clearly more influenced by the inertia of received opinions than by any new assessment of British policy [34]. Bevin's biographer, Lord Bullock, has put forward a different view. In his opinion, the crucial turning-point 'came in 1955–7 [with Messina and the EEC*] not 1950'. By 1955, the British government had had a chance to see what the Europeans were doing, to re-assess Britain's position in the world, and to realise that Britain could not 'lead' from outside. Moreover, Britain clearly had a greater interest in proposals for a general common market than in a community for coal and steel [64 *p. 784*]. A third interpretation was put forward by Lord Sherfield, who as Sir Roger Makins was an important influence on British policy at the time. In his view, the 'wait and see' policy was essentially correct. By the time Britain did apply to join the European Communities (in 1961), it was in 'very different circumstances' from 1950 or 1955: 'the "federal" implications had been much diminished', and 'the economic and industrial failure of the United Kingdom in the 1960s' was now discernible [34 *p. 117*].

Other historians have argued not that it was right or wrong, but that it was inevitable that British governments should have taken the decisions that they did [38, 45]. In Britain, there was no real European 'movement' to speak of, by comparison with 'the Six'. Public opinion was largely indifferent: not hostile, but certainly not positive [73, 99]. The 'three circles' approach required that Britain should not become exclusively attached to any one of the three. The relationship with America was complicated by American policy-makers' persistent attempts to persuade Britain to take a more active role in Europe, but British policy-makers believed that the relationship would no longer be 'special' if Britain were 'merely ... a potential unit of a Federated Europe' [2 *p. 115*]. Britain's relationship with the empire and Commonwealth remained another significant brake on integration with Europe. Politically, it was still expected that the Commonwealth would play a major role in world affairs. Economically, the Commonwealth remained far more important to Britain than was Europe [38 *pp. 59–60*].

John Young has put forward the view that the failure to establish close co-operation between Britain and Europe was 'also due to the refusal of the continentals' [104 *p. 131*]. The French government, in particular, frequently acted in such a way as to exclude Britain, and Monnet believed that it was better to make a start without Britain, for fear that otherwise the principle of supranationality would be sacrificed. Britain would join Europe 'when you see that we've succeeded'. [34 *p. 166*, 19]. The extent to which Britain could have determined the shape of Europe's new institutions by joining earlier is of course debatable. The essential motor always was the Franco–German axis. British attempts to set the agenda (as by Bevin in 1946–48) elicited little enthusiasm on the continent, and were rapidly eclipsed [38, 45].

THE SUEZ CRISIS

During the latter half of 1956, Britain's and the world's attention was focused not on the continuing negotiations in Brussels but on Egypt, where the regime of Colonel Nasser precipitated a crisis with the West by nationalising the Suez Canal. Britain and France (the two countries with major stakes in the Suez Canal Company) concluded a secret agreement with Israel leading to an invasion of the canal zone. The spectacle of old-fashioned imperialism aroused enormous indignation within the international community and within British (but less so French) domestic opinion. When the crisis precipitated a run on the pound, America made it clear that it would not help while British troops were still in Egypt. On 3 December, much to France's chagrin, Eden announced British withdrawal. Eden himself was forced to resign a few weeks later.

The consequences of Suez for French policy were relatively clear: it confirmed the unreliability of the British and the necessity of taking a lead in European integration in order to remain a world player [30 *pp. 154–5*]. A number of historians have argued that in the long term Suez contributed to a similar shift in British orientation towards Europe. Eden certainly believed that one consequence of the crisis would be 'to determine us to work more closely with Europe' [6 *pp. 87–8*]. As far as the Commonwealth (which was deeply divided) was concerned, Suez was a 'psychological watershed' which led to 'a hastening of the removal of the vestiges of Britain's imperial statehood, a diminishing pride in the Commonwealth ... and a willingness to reduce or shed the role of principal in Commonwealth affairs' [96 *p. 272*]. Nevertheless, the effects of the crisis were 'not obvious, simple, clear-cut or immediate' [11 *p. 231*]. While many in Britain thought the Suez invasion had been wrong, many others thought that it had merely been mishandled. It was not until 1968 that Britain finally decided to pull out from its imperial and military commitments 'east of Suez'. In the short term, the government's priority was to re-forge its links with America and the Commonwealth and restore Britain's international prestige.

4 MACMILLAN AND THE FIRST APPLICATION, 1957–64

Macmillan's reputation for political adeptness verging on Machiavellianism was enhanced by the circumstances of his coming to power. On Suez he had been 'first in, first out', as Harold Wilson observed [118 *p. 113*]. He turned the crisis to his advantage, and smartly outmanoeuvred his rival for the succession, Rab Butler [112]. Nevertheless, Macmillan was also a man of principle and of pronounced pro-European views. He had fought and lost many friends in the First World War, opposed appeasement, and in 1939 called for 'an organisation, economic, cultural, and perhaps even political, comprising all the countries of western Europe' [97 *p. 152*]. After the war, he had been prominent in the European Movement and a leading 'Strasbourger'. That it was his government which launched Britain's first bid to join the European Communities (the ECSC, the EEC and the European Atomic Energy Community (Euratom)*) in 1961 has been seen by many commentators as pre-eminently the outcome of his leadership on the issue [106, 107]. However, concentration on Macmillan's key role should not obscure the convergence of pressures to which he was reacting; nor should it ignore the fact that his policy went through many convolutions before 1961, and that even after then he was ambivalent in terms of his commitment to Europe.

MESSINA TO BRUSSELS (VIA ROME)

The British *démarche* from the Spaak negotiations at the end of 1955 caused considerable resentment amongst 'the Six', especially as it was accompanied by underhand attempts to persuade the German and American governments to oppose the idea of a common market and by a British initiative to bring the negotiations within the OEEC. Britain's diplomacy left a legacy of suspicion and distrust and served only to unite 'the Six'. The Spaak committee reported in April 1956 and the following month, at Venice, 'the Six' agreed to draw up treaties embodying the report's proposals. It was Venice, rather than Messina, which forced a significant shift in British thinking. It was now clear that 'the Six' meant business [113]. Macmillan (then Chancellor) instructed the Treasury to draw up various strategies for dealing with the emergent European bloc. Of these, the Cabinet chose 'Plan G': a proposal for an industrial free trade area linking 'the Six' with the other eleven OEEC members. The plan deliberately excluded agriculture and allowed member-states to set their own tariffs against non-members (unlike the EEC). Macmillan insisted that the latter was fundamental: Britain could never agree 'to our entering arrangements which, as a matter of principle, would prevent our treating the great range of imports from the Commonwealth at least as favourably as those from the European countries' [8, 26 Nov. 1956, cols 37–8]. Macmillan's proposal was, as he later admitted, an attempt to get the best of all worlds [115 *pp. 80–8*]. Understandably, the Europeans were unenthused. The French, in particular, suspected another attempt to undermine the common market negotiations.

On 25 March 1957 the leaders of 'the Six' signed the two Treaties of Rome,* establishing the European Economic Community (EEC) (the 'common market') and Euratom. The two new Communities came into existence on 1 January 1958, sharing the ECSC's Assembly, Council and Court, but with separate and less powerful Commissions.* (The latter merged with the ECSC's High Authority in 1967.) The EEC Treaty was by far the more significant of the two, envisaging the abolition of internal customs duties, the erection of a common external tariff, free movement of capital and labour, the progressive integration of policies in areas such as agriculture, transport, trade and competition, and the gradual realisation of an 'ever closer union' among the member-states. The first round of tariff adjustments was scheduled for 1 January 1959.

The emergence of a potentially powerful economic bloc at the heart of western Europe filled a number of Cabinet ministers with dismay. David Eccles declared, embarrassingly, that twice within living memory Britain had gone to war to oppose the formation of 'a hostile bloc across the Channel' [111 *p. 39*]. A year later, Macmillan contemplated withdrawing from NATO and 'fight[ing] back with every weapon in our armoury' if 'the Six' rejected the free trade area [*Doc. 6b*]. Nevertheless, it soon became clear that 'the Six' were uninterested in any proposal which excluded agriculture and external tariffs, and also that they wanted access to Commonwealth markets on equal terms with Britain. Nor was the British proposal attractive to many other countries. It was estimated that 80 per cent of Denmark's exports would still face tariffs, while 90 per cent of its imports would not. The negotiations had already run into the ground by the time they were ended, in November 1958, by de Gaulle, who had returned to power as Prime Minister in June, and who was about to become President of France for the next eleven years [108, 112].

EEC AND EFTA

The Conservatives' threats of retaliation failed to materialise. Nevertheless, the prospect of a trade war was a powerful inducement to Britain to join with Austria, Denmark, Norway, Portugal, Sweden and Switzerland in negotiating the European Free Trade Association (EFTA),* as an alternative to the EEC. EFTA represented a considerable modification of Britain's original free trade area proposal in the interests of the Danes and others, and came into existence on 1 January 1960. Miriam Camps has argued that it was a sincere attempt to maintain the unity of western Europe and advanced a considerable way towards European integration [108]. However, most historians have seen it as no more than a side-show, or a cul-de-sac on the route to British membership of the EEC. It was conceived as an expedient and supported by the British government primarily to improve its bargaining position with 'the Six'. The economic benefits went mainly to Sweden and Switzerland. Over the first three years of its existence, British exports to EFTA countries rose by 33 per cent. Over the same period, British exports to EEC countries (now facing escalating tariffs) rose by 55 per cent [112 *p. 131*]. The American administration made clear its unfavourable view of EFTA, which it regarded as embodying all of the economic costs to America but none of the political benefits of the EEC [111 *p. 45*]. In the short term, EFTA failed to fulfil its role as a 'bridge-builder': the EEC countries refused to take it seriously. In the medium term, it was a diplomatic own-goal for Britain, as it set up another major obstacle to membership of the EEC [119].

The EEC, by contrast, enjoyed rapid success. Despite British protests, the programme of tariff adjustments was accelerated and the first Commission under Walter Hallstein produced a series of successful initiatives in other areas of integration. With the exception of Belgium, the EEC countries enjoyed economic growth rates much higher than Britain's [17, 22]. While it is not possible to say that this was the result of EEC membership, Britain's non-membership threatened to exclude it from some of the world's major growth markets, and to leave it dependent on the Commonwealth, whose economies were increasingly successful at competing with British goods [20].

TOWARDS THE FIRST APPLICATION

Changing trade patterns were a major factor in impelling Britain towards membership of the EEC. Even the Commonwealth Relations Office concluded, in 1956, that Britain's trade with the Commonwealth was in long-term decline [113 *pp. 128–9*]. Nevertheless, the same year, the authors of 'Plan G' noted that 'less than one-third of our trade is with Europe; entry into a common market would be bound to damage much of the other two-thirds (particularly that with the Commonwealth)' [112 *p. 92*]. It was not until after Britain had actually joined the European Communities, in the 1970s, that British trade with Europe overtook that with the Commonwealth [141 *pp. 193–4*].

It is now generally agreed that political rather than economic factors were uppermost in the minds of Macmillan and his colleagues as they moved towards launching an application [38, 45]. The role of public opinion is unclear, although there is some evidence of a groundswell amongst 'informed' business and media circles [99]. Macmillan himself was influenced by events on the wider stage. He signalled his acceptance that the days of empire were coming to an end with his 'wind of change' speech in February 1960, and the illusions of those who thought the Commonwealth was a vehicle for British influence were punctured by Britain's increasing isolation on the question of South Africa [11]. The decline in Britain's international standing was accentuated by the collapse of the Blue Streak weapons programme: Britain was forced into dependence on America in order to maintain its 'independent' nuclear deterrent. Macmillan's private secretary later recalled that the failure of the May 1960 superpower summit, which Macmillan had worked hard to bring about, was the crucial turning-point. Then, he found that the United States could treat Britain as 'just another power' [34 *p. 237*]. The danger that 'the Six' might supplant Britain as 'the second member of the North Atlantic Alliance', and that the 'pull of this new power bloc would be bound to dilute our influence with the rest of the world' was highlighted by an influential Cabinet committee later the same month [*Doc. 7a*]. A number of historians have concluded that Britain's application to join the EEC was an attempt to restore its deteriorating position in all three of Churchill's 'circles' [11 *p. 234*, 37 *p. 44*].

Soundings with European governments soon established that there would be no halfway house between full membership and exclusion, and in May 1960 Macmillan decided that Britain should consider joining the EEC as a full member. There then followed an extraordinary display of Macmillan's political skill, which ensured that he was able to reverse established Conservative policy within a year without 'losing the smallest parliamentary Secretary or Junior Whip along the way' [106 *p. 10*]. Supporters of British entry were put in key posts – Sandys at Commonwealth Relations, Christopher Soames at Agriculture – and Edward Heath was appointed Lord Privy Seal, with responsibility for any negotiations. Sceptics, such as Butler and Reginald Maudling, were neutralised. Behind the scenes, Macmillan prepared the ground, winning the support of President Kennedy and putting out feelers to 'the Six'. France was identified as the one potential opponent. In February 1961 the Foreign Office reported that 'not much common ground was found' in exploratory talks, and the following month the Paris Embassy reported that de Gaulle had set up a committee 'to think up ways of keeping us out' [112 *pp. 141–4*]. Nevertheless, Macmillan hoped that de Gaulle might be won over by promises of nuclear know-how, and by the prospect of gaining an ally in his fight against supranationalism within the Communities. Even if this failed, he still hoped to out-manoeuvre de Gaulle [45, 112]. Thus it was that on 31 July 1961, Macmillan announced in the House of Commons (which was about to break up for the long summer break) that Britain would be seeking negotiations on the terms of British membership.

THE BRUSSELS NEGOTIATIONS

Given the magnitude of the issue, Macmillan's announcement was surprisingly low-key. There was no indication of any decisive shift in British policy. Indeed, a number of authors have concluded that Macmillan made a fatal mistake by tying the success of the negotiations to the satisfaction of British interests in three problematic areas: the Commonwealth, EFTA and British agriculture [27, 108, 109]. Heath, in his opening statement to 'the Six' in October 1961, was more enthusiastic: Britain, he declared, was willing 'to subscribe fully to the aims which you have set yourselves'. The problems raised by British entry, he believed, were 'in no way insuperable' [*Doc. 7b*]. Heath's assessment in fact proved wildly over-optimistic, and the problems identified by Macmillan not only dominated the Brussels negotiations but also engendered a heated debate in Britain. Macmillan's conditions were, in a very real sense, hostages to fortune.

The problems faced by Heath and his team of negotiators were compounded by the fact that the debate in Britain accompanied rather than preceded the negotiations; by the necessity of parallel negotiations with the Commonwealth and EFTA; and also by the difficulty of negotiating when certain key issues (notably the Common Agricultural Policy* and political union) were still themselves the subject of negotiations between 'the Six'. Heath complained that he sometimes felt he was having to negotiate on a 'moving belt'. Given the obstacles, it is perhaps remarkable that the negotiations proceeded as far as they did [108, 109].

The problem of agriculture proved unexpectedly difficult. British agricultural policy differed fundamentally from that eventually adopted by 'the Six' in January 1962, in that Britain maintained an open market for agricultural products and protected farmers by a system of deficiency payments, whereas 'the Six' threw the burden primarily on the consumer by maintaining high prices through import levies and export subsidies. The British government had already made clear that the British system was becoming too costly and would have to change, but the CAP seemed in many respects worse – as the major food importer, Britain would effectively be subsidising farmers in the rest of the Community [114].

EFTA also proved a particularly thorny issue. By the 'London Agreement' of June 1961, Britain rashly agreed not to enter the EEC until the interests of the other six EFTA members were secured. However, it soon became clear that 'the Six' would not negotiate with EFTA *en bloc*. Denmark applied for EEC membership shortly after Britain, but the form of 'association' sought by the other EFTA members had yet to be discussed when the Brussels negotiations ended. It was clear, nevertheless, that in order to join the EEC Britain might have to renege on the 'London Agreement' [119].

The most important obstacle to British membership – in terms of the scale of the problem, its capacity to arouse British opinion, and the difficulty of reconciling British interests with those of 'the Six' – was the Commonwealth. As a result of last-minute pressure, France had managed to gain special status for all its 'overseas territories'; but it was made clear from the beginning that the EEC could not accommodate the Commonwealth in the same way. The negotiations got off to a bad start in July 1961 when Heath and four other ministers toured Commonwealth capitals and encountered a storm of hostility to Britain's application. This was confirmed by a meeting of Commonwealth finance ministers at Accra in September, who issued a statement which reflected the unease felt in Commonwealth countries at the possible danger to their interests and warned that British entry would inevitably weaken the Commonwealth as a whole. At first the British negotiators in Brussels attempted to deal with Commonwealth problems in five broad categories: raw materials, high-wage-cost manufactures, low-wage-cost manufactures, temperate agriculture and tropical agriculture. As the negotiations proceeded, these categories were further broken down, on a country-by-country and product-by-product basis. By the time negotiations ended, it seemed that agreements were in sight for some special items (New Zealand butter, Indian handloom products, etc.) but that the most 'the Six' would offer for the broad range of Commonwealth goods (but not for low-wage-cost manufactures) was a more gradual imposition of the external tariff. From what they knew of the Brussels terms at the time of their meeting in London, in September 1962, the Commonwealth prime ministers were not encouraged: indeed, their final communiqué noted 'the extent to which their interests had not so far been met' [108 *p. 443*, 109].

Despite upbeat reports from Heath and others, news of the progress of the Brussels negotiations tended also to exacerbate domestic opposition to membership. Macmillan was able to contain opposition within his own party, although there is evidence that unease in the parliamentary party as well as at grass-roots was growing [99, 107]. He has often been criticised, however, for failing to gain all-party support for such a major innovation in foreign policy [106, 108]. Initially, the Labour Party was fairly evenly divided. Its leader, Hugh Gaitskell, held the party together by insisting on the same three conditions as Macmillan, and two more (Britain's right to undertake economic planning, and its continued independence in foreign policy). As Philip Williams has observed, 'terms good enough to enable Macmillan to carry his own party would also allow Gaitskell to carry his; and without such terms the talks would collapse and Labour could only benefit' [122 *p. 706*]. Gaitskell himself appeared to believe that the terms would be met and that membership would be in Britain's interest. Nevertheless, the Commonwealth was 'really the nub of the whole question'. For Gaitskell, the turning-point was the meeting of Commonwealth leaders in London in September [122 *p. 722*]. In a broadcast at the end of the month, he declared that membership of the EEC would mean 'the end of Britain as an independent nation … the end of a thousand years of history'. He repeated his message in a rousing speech to the Labour Party conference the following month [*Doc. 7c*].

There is abundant evidence to show that public opinion was moving against British membership in the latter half of 1962. Labour enjoyed a surge in popularity, opinion polls showed clear majorities against joining, and pressure groups such as the Anti-Common Market League far outpaced the pro-European groups [99, 110]. The shift in British opinion, and the possibility that an anti-market Labour government would be returned at the next election, may have been factors in de Gaulle's decision effectively to veto Britain's application, which he announced at a press conference on 14 January 1963. Certainly, he emphasised that Britain did not seem committed to Europe. For him, this had a particular meaning: Britain was too committed to the Commonwealth and the United States. His own vision of Europe as a 'third force' would be fatally undermined by the entry of Britain, which he regarded as an American 'Trojan Horse' – especially after the Nassau agreement of December 1962, which allowed Britain to buy American Polaris missiles. Nuclear politics thus 'muddied hopelessly the waters of the British application' [109 *p. 53*]. Nevertheless, de Gaulle was almost certainly intent on wrecking the British application before Nassau, and was merely awaiting his opportunity [121]. His critique of Britain's application went deep: in his view, 'the nature, the structure, the very situation' of Britain made it fundamentally different from the continent [*Doc. 7d*].

BRITAIN OUTSIDE EUROPE

The British government was at first unsure how to react to de Gaulle's statement. It was hoped that the leaders of the five other EEC countries would prevail on de Gaulle, but, while there was considerable sympathy for Britain, none of the five was prepared to threaten the fragile unity of 'the Six'. Germany even proceeded to sign a Treaty of Friendship with France. By the end of January, it was clear the negotiations would get nowhere. Heath withdrew from Brussels, but by no means in bitterness. 'We are not going to turn our backs on ... Europe', he declared. 'We are a part of Europe: by geography, tradition, history, culture and civilization' [108 *p. 492*]. Macmillan, in the House of Commons, claimed that the negotiations had been broken off 'not ... because the discussions were menaced with failure', but 'because they threatened to succeed' [117, *p. 377*]. Historians have differed as to whether he was correct. The Commission President, Walter Hallstein, thought that he was not. In his view, Britain would have to make important further concessions in order to secure membership. Macmillan was at least spared the difficult business of getting such concessions accepted at home [108, 112].

De Gaulle's veto was 'a blow to the prestige of the Macmillan Government from which the Conservatives did not really recover' [112 *p*. 9]. Macmillan himself soldiered on – hoping for a change of heart in Europe, without optimism or immediate reason – until the Profumo scandal brought him down in October 1963. His successor, Alec Douglas-Home, went to the polls a year later, and was narrowly (but decisively) beaten. Most writers have argued that Britain's first application came too late: Britain had already missed the European boat [28, 34, 108]. In the opinion of Gaitskell and de Gaulle, however, the application came too early. This view is supported by George Wilkes, who has argued that Britain was not yet ready to make the adjustments necessitated by EEC membership, while the EEC itself was still too young to accommodate the changes which British membership at that time might have entailed [120].

5   WILSON AND THE SECOND APPLICATION, 1964–70

Hugh Gaitskell having died early in 1963, it was his successor as leader of the Labour Party, Harold Wilson, who took office as Prime Minister in October 1964. By repute, Wilson was a left-winger. This reputation certainly helped him secure the leadership. Nevertheless, as a number of historians have emphasised, his track record in government was that of a pragmatist, a 'compromiser', even an 'opportunist' [130, 131]. Chris Wrigley has argued that foreign policy was one area where Wilson was given ample opportunity to display his 'considerable short-term political skills'. By a series of manoeuvres and initiatives 'he not only deflected attention away from other serious problems, both international and domestic, but also heightened expectations of Britain's influence in world affairs' [134 *p. 123*]. The need for Wilson's 'magic' was considerably greater after the October 1964 election, when Labour was returned with a majority of five (soon reduced to three), than after the March 1966 election, when Labour increased its majority to 97. Indeed, Wilson's 1964–66 government appears in retrospect to have been much more successful than that of 1966–70.

LABOUR AND EUROPE

On Europe, Wilson appears to have been an agnostic. In 1961–62 he equivocated, seeing both opportunities and dangers for Britain in EEC membership, but he followed Gaitskell's lead in declaring the likely terms of entry unacceptable in October 1962. As leader of the opposition, he frequently taunted the government for its lack of constructive alternatives to a further EEC application. Much of this style followed him into government. In a speech during the 1966 election, following hints of a re-assessment in French policy, he commented, 'now one encouraging gesture from the French Government ... and the Conservative leader [Edward Heath] rolls on his back like a spaniel'. Nevertheless, in the same speech, he declared that, 'given the right conditions', a Labour government might consider joining [127 *p. 199;* 131 *p. 397*]. Ben Pimlott has argued that, to the extent that Wilson had a particular orientation in foreign policy, his 'personal preference was for a new emphasis on the Commonwealth' [131 *p. 433*]. Europe was not an issue on which he had strong opinions. Indeed, he tended to see the question of EEC membership primarily in relation to other, to him more important, problems, such as that of maintaining Labour Party unity under his own leadership [131].

Wilson's non-committal attitude towards Europe was a necessary one during 1964–66, and Labour's narrow parliamentary majority ensured his success in keeping both supporters and opponents of EEC membership in line. The parliamentary party was divided roughly three ways: one-third favouring a positive approach to Europe, one-third opposing membership on any likely terms, and one-third either uninterested or unconvinced. Left-wingers were prominent opponents of the EEC, seeing it as a 'capitalist club'. Nevertheless, the issue cut across the traditional issues dividing left and right in the Labour Party. The right-wing Douglas Jay opposed membership, perceiving a threat to Britain's Atlantic commitment; the left-wing Anthony Wedgwood (Tony) Benn supported membership, partly out of anti-Americanism and partly out of a hope that it would improve British prospects in the new technologies. Wilson's Cabinet reflected these various currents of opinion. Wilson's first Foreign Secretary, Patrick Gordon-Walker, was 'a Commonwealth man' and an Atlanticist, who believed that Britain should treat the EEC simply as a 'neighbour ... with whom we need good relations' [45 *p. 86*]. His successor, Michael Stewart, was equally attached to the Atlantic alliance: indeed, on the major issue in foreign policy, the Vietnam conflict, he 'became a more convincing exponent of the US case than some of the American leaders' [134 *p. 129*]. Nevertheless, Stewart 'became more pro-European as time went on', under pressure from George Brown (deputy leader of the party and head of the Department of Economic Affairs) and from pro-European officials in the Foreign Office [45 *p. 88*].

After de Gaulle's veto in 1963, Macmillan noted in his diary, 'the great question remains, "What is the alternative?" to the European Community. If we are honest, we must say there is none' [117 *p. 374*]. Robert Lieber has similarly described Labour's 'progress towards Europe' as 'a story of collapsing alternatives' [41 *p. 261*]. Wilson won the 1964 election with vague promises about new initiatives to promote Commonwealth trade, EFTA and even a free trade area covering virtually the whole of the developed world. He was

adamant that Britain would remain 'a world power, and a world influence, or we are nothing' [14 *p. 226*]. Yet within little more than
two years he (like Macmillan) was reduced to 'trailing round Europe
with a begging bowl' [131 *p. 443*].

Labour's proposals for increasing Commonwealth trade proved to
be little more than a 'pipe dream' [132 *p. 77*]. The long-term decline
in British-Commonwealth trade continued, and even accelerated, as
Commonwealth countries (especially Canada and Australia) diversi-
fied their trade in the wake of Britain's 1961–63 turn to Europe.
Britain's disengagement from the Commonwealth continued, as evi-
denced by its agreement to the creation of a Commonwealth
Secretariat separate from the British government. For the British government, the Commonwealth's political value was reduced by the rise
of the non-aligned movement, by the Commonwealth's failure to
mediate in the Indo-Pakistan dispute of 1965, and by increasing
Commonwealth criticism of Britain for its support of undemocratic
regimes in South Africa, Rhodesia, Guyana and later Nigeria. The
January 1966 Commonwealth Prime Ministers' meeting in Lagos was
a disaster for Britain. Richard Crossman wrote that the Commonwealth was 'fading out' [125 *p. 30*]. He was wrong, of course; but he
would have been right to describe the government's commitment to
the Commonwealth as 'fading out'.

In 1966–67 there was much talk of a North Atlantic Free Trade
Area (NAFTA), a proposal put forward by Senator J. Javits of America. Wilson's government undertook studies of the proposal, but soon
found that President Johnson's administration was unfavourable to
the idea (which would have offered America few advantages by comparison with the disadvantages of increased competition in the
American market). Instead, Johnson pushed forward the 'Kennedy
round' of General Agreement on Tariffs and Trade (GATT)* negotiations, in which Britain found itself significantly disadvantaged in
comparison with the EEC. American pressure on Britain to join Europe continued, while at the same time British influence with the
American administration declined. The 'special' relationship was
strained by Wilson's reluctance to support America in Vietnam, and
by the ever-present (although for Wilson odious) possibility that
economic weakness would force Britain to withdraw its military
presence 'east of Suez'.

EFTA was, of course, no alternative to the EEC – especially after
the failure of another attempt at 'bridge-building' with 'the Six' in
1965. GITA ('going it alone') was also considered, but by February
1966 Wilson had decided that 'the difficulties of staying outside Eu-

rope and surviving as an independent power are very great compared with entering on the right conditions' [124 *p. 461*].

The gravitational pull of Europe was becoming considerable. The EEC hastened its programme of tariff adjustments, completing the customs union in July 1968. Europe's market of 250 million consumers was thus increasingly closed to Britain, where economic growth continued to lag far behind. Taking the years 1960–70 as a whole, the GNP of 'the Six' increased by an average of 4.2 per cent a year, compared with 2.3 per cent in Britain. At the same time, changes in the Communities themselves made membership a more attractive option. Britain's worries about the impact of EEC membership on the more vulnerable Commonwealth states were lessened after the first Yaoundé* agreement, which gave considerable guarantees to the ex-colonial territories of 'the Six'. Britain's worries about supranationalism were lessened by de Gaulle's boycott of Community institutions, which lasted from July 1965 until January 1966, and resulted in the 'Luxembourg compromise',* whereby any member-state could effectively veto any proposal on the grounds of national interest. De Gaulle's boycott was partly prompted by disagreements over the financing of the Common Agricultural Policy. That decisions would nevertheless have to be reached was a consideration that in 1965–67 pointed to an early British application, if Britain were to apply at all.

ECONOMIC DECLINE

Wilson's 1964 election campaign had been resonant with images of modernisation and of the new Britain to be forged in the 'white heat' of the 'scientific revolution'. Actual commitments were harder to find. This was perhaps wise. Labour inherited what a Labour supporter has described as a 'grave but not critical' economic situation from the Conservatives, which it then proceeded to make worse [132 *p. 25*].

The crux of the problem was the pressure on the pound caused by the balance of payments deficit (i.e., the gap between imports and exports), now reaching alarming levels. The causes of this were long term and plentiful, including over-reliance on declining industries, lack of investment, and low productivity. In the short term, there were three solutions: import controls, deflation (i.e., reducing the amount of money in circulation) and devaluation (reducing the value of sterling). Import controls were largely ruled out by international agreement and the threat of retaliation. Britain could not afford to retreat into a siege economy because its economic existence was dependent to an unusual extent on foreign trade. Deflation was another non-starter. The price would be huge public expenditure cuts, unemployment at 1930s levels and the possible eclipse of Harold Wilson and the Labour Party. Devaluation was the third possibility. Although Brown and other colleagues came to see devaluation as the key to economic growth, Wilson adamantly refused to repeat the experience of 1949 and turn Labour into 'the party of devaluation'. 'Devaluation would sweep us away. We would have to go to the country defeated' [124 *p. 71*]. Instead, Labour negotiated a $2 billion loan from the US. This merely postponed the day of reckoning. Meanwhile, the balance of payments sank further into deficit, both unemployment and inflation rose, strikes became more widespread and the economy lurched from one crisis to another [132].

The worst crisis came in July 1966, when a national seamen's strike, compounding a depressing set of economic indicators, triggered a severe run on the pound. Brown urged a decisive change of policy. 'We've got to break with America, devalue and go into Europe' [123 *p. 148*]. Wilson suspected an attempt to undermine his own position. As John Young has pointed out, he 'was able to exploit "anti-market" sentiments to defeat Brown', but this 'did not mean that Wilson opposed EEC membership; it meant that he hoped to achieve membership *without* a prior devaluation' [45 *p. 93*]. He now accepted the case for devaluation, but he recognised that it would be more acceptable to the British public and the international money markets if it were part of a whole package of measures, including membership of the EEC. The race was therefore on, to join the EEC before being forced to devalue outside. A story went the rounds in London at this time, that Macmillan had left a black box in Downing Street, to be opened by a future prime minister in a moment of despair. Inside was a simple message: 'Join the Common Market' [127].

THE SECOND BRITISH APPLICATION

A whole host of reasons conspired to edge Wilson towards launching a second British application: changes in the international sphere, changes in the Communities themselves, the hope of reversing Britain's economic decline and the need to find a framework for the inevitable devaluation. Added to this were pressures from the Foreign Office, the Confederation of British Industries, much of the press and European-minded pressure groups. There was also evidence of widespread public support for British membership. In mid-1966 opinion polls found 70 per cent of respondents in favour of joining the 'com-

mon market' [126]. Party politics also pointed to a renewed application. The March 1966 election gave Wilson more leeway to adopt
controversial policies, but it also made difficult choices more necessary, by unbottling Labour Party in-fighting. A large number of the
new intake of Labour MPs were known to be pro-European. Moreover, Wilson was attracted by the thought of scotching the
Conservatives by stealing their trump card. Finally, a foreign policy
'miracle' was needed to distract attention from difficulties with the
economy and in other foreign policy areas [129, 134].

Like contemporaries, historians have been unable to discover exactly when Wilson finally changed his mind on EEC membership. Some
have argued that he had already done so before the 1964 election,
others that he did so only just before the 1966 election. In John
Young's judgement, 'the most convincing interpretation of the evidence points to Wilson becoming more "pro-European" in 1964–66.
The reason he could not be more forthright on the issue was that he
needed to keep the Cabinet united until a healthy majority was
achieved' [45 *p. 88–9*]. The 1966 manifesto registered a subtle but
important shift in Labour's policy, by declaring that Britain would be
ready to enter Europe 'provided essential ... interests are safeguarded'
[45 *p. 91*]. Immediately after the election, Wilson appointed the pro-
European George Thomson 'Minister for Europe', and instituted a
Cabinet committee to review European policy. The sterling crisis of
July 1966 accelerated his manoeuvres, and in August he appointed
Brown Foreign Secretary. (Stewart, by now a firm pro-European,
took over the Department of Economic Affairs.)

Towards the end of October 1966, the Cabinet met at Chequers for
a weekend session to discuss Britain's European policy. Wilson was
careful to emphasise that he was in favour of keeping all options
open, but he was able to win support for the idea of a 'probe' by
Brown and himself, in the form of a visit to each of the governments
of 'the Six'. A number of ministers had serious doubts about the initiative, but they agreed to let it go forward, hoping, in Richard
Crossman's words, that in the last resort 'the General will save us
from our own folly' [45 *p. 95*]. Amidst mounting press and parliamentary speculation, Wilson announced the 'probe' to the Commons
on 10 November. Ben Pimlott has observed that Wilson 'found it
hard to be a half-hearted salesman' [131 *p. 439*]. It is true that from
this point on Wilson's references to Europe gained an unaccustomed
enthusiasm. In a speech of 14 November, Wilson decisively rejected
the 'little England philosophy', and painted a roseate picture of
Anglo-European collaboration. In the same speech, he also intro-

duced the idea of a fourth, 'European Technological' Community [*Doc. 8a*].

The Wilson/Brown tour duly opened discussions with the governments of 'the Six', revealing considerable enthusiasm for British membership amongst the 'Friendly Five', but continuing reservations on the part of France. 'Was it possible for Britain at present – and was Britain willing? – to follow any policy that was really distinct from that of the United States', de Gaulle asked. Wilson had no answer; nevertheless, he returned convinced that he had managed to overawe de Gaulle [131 *p. 441*]. A series of Cabinet meetings followed, during which the pro-marketeers were joined by Crossman (who now saw membership as the means to devaluation) and James Callaghan (whose experience as Chancellor had convinced him that national sovereignty was a figment). On 2 May 1967, Wilson announced the government's intention to apply for membership. A week later there followed a three-day Commons debate. The result (488 to 62 in favour of the application) was never in doubt, given that the front benches of all three major parties supported the proposal [127, 129].

With the debate for the moment settled in Britain, the focus shifted to Europe. De Gaulle was universally recognised as the major obstacle to British membership. On 16 May he held a press conference in Paris, in which, while avoiding the question of whether he would actually veto the British application, he made clear that he still objected to British entry. In particular, he believed that Britain would be a 'Trojan horse' for America, because of their strong links in defence – France had meanwhile pulled out of the NATO integrated command – and American support for sterling. Moreover, de Gaulle now raised the question of whether Britain's economy was so weak that British membership would harm the existing 'Six' and he insisted that Britain should end sterling's role as a reserve currency [30, 121]. In June, Wilson attempted to win over de Gaulle by another personal visit. He returned disappointed, but determined 'not ... to take no for an answer', hoping that progress in the negotiations would make a veto unacceptable to the 'Friendly Five'. The negotiations, which started in July, did make swift progress, largely because the British, learning from their 1961–63 experience, kept their conditions to a minimum. Commonwealth obstacles were reduced to a British request for special arrangements for Caribbean sugar and New Zealand lamb and dairy products. The CAP was accepted in full (although Britain requested changes in the financing arrangements so far agreed). Denmark, Ireland and Norway also applied to join the Communities. For the other EFTA countries, Britain requested only a year's transitional arrangements [127, 129].

De Gaulle's hand was strengthened first by a European Commission report of September 1967, which recommended that Britain should resolve its balance of payments problem and end sterling's role as a reserve currency before joining the Communities, and secondly, far more spectacularly, by the devaluation which was forced on Britain on 18 November. He wasted little time. At a press conference at the Elysée palace on 27 November, he declared that there was still 'a very vast and deep mutation to be effected' by Britain before France could accept it as a fellow-member of the Communities [*Doc. 8b*]. De Gaulle's press conference effectively ended the second British application. Wilson attempted to drive a wedge between the 'Friendly Five' and the French leader but to little avail. Largely out of bureaucratic tidiness, the French issued a formal veto on 16 May 1968 [129].

BRITAIN IN WAITING

Rather than withdrawing its application, as in 1963, the British government left it 'on the table', to be re-activated whenever 'the Six' saw fit. This effectively meant when de Gaulle was either dead or gone. For other reasons, the issue of British membership lost its urgency. The 'pro-Europeans' lost their most powerful champion in March 1968, when Brown resigned – largely in protest at Wilson's style of government. The British economy showed a marked improvement as a result of devaluation and of Roy Jenkins's firm leadership as Chancellor. Britain's withdrawal from 'east of Suez' – which Wilson was finally forced to accept as a concomitant of devaluation – also helped to restore confidence in Britain's finances. Ironically, it was de Gaulle, fatally weakened by the civil disturbances of May 1968, who approached Britain in February 1969, with an offer to recast the EEC as an intergovernmental free trade area, with Britain as a member. Perhaps out of revenge for the two humiliating vetoes the Foreign Office took the unprecedented step of communicating to France's partners a report of de Gaulle's approach. The affair added to de Gaulle's troubles. Three months later he at last resigned [30, 121].

De Gaulle's successor, Georges Pompidou, was a Gaullist, but significantly more favourable to the European Communities, and more open to British membership, than de Gaulle himself. Indeed, he saw Britain as a potential counterweight to Germany, now the economic giant of the Communities. Pompidou's anxieties were increased after the election of Willy Brandt as German Chancellor in September 1969. Brandt was committed to a policy of *Ostpolitik*, i.e., the opening-up of relations with the eastern bloc. Like previous chancellors, however, Brandt conceived of the Communities as the essential framework for German policy. Again like previous chancellors, he favoured both the deepening of the Communities through further integration and the enlargement of the Communities to include Britain and other EFTA members. At the Hague summit of December 1969, the Franco–German axis produced a remarkable leap forward. Britain and the other applicants were invited to resume negotiations, provided that they 'accept the treaties and their political finality' and 'the decisions taken since the entry into force of the treaties' (the so-called *acquis communautaire*). Agreement was also reached on the principles of CAP financing: import duties on non-EEC agricultural products and 1 per cent of Value Added Tax were to constitute the Community's 'own resources'. The common market was to be extended to further areas of economic activity. Finally, a start was to be made on Economic and Monetary Union (EMU),* with an agreement to use currency reserves to limit exchange-rate fluctuations.

The Labour government, still buoyed by indications of economic progress, and mindful of the party politics of the issue, recognised the Hague proposals to be a mixed offering. The financial arrangements agreed for CAP looked certain to ensure that Britain (as a major food importer) would pay far more in duties and VAT than (with a relatively small agricultural sector) it would ever receive in subsidies. The proposal of monetary union was also unwelcome, given that sterling was affected by worldwide movements far more than the franc or the mark. Wilson's government published a White Paper in February 1970, showing that entry under existing conditions would mean a balance of payments drain of £1 billion a year, and food on average 25 per cent dearer. The White Paper's figures were disputed, and 'could have been designed to strengthen Britain's negotiating position for tough bargaining with the Six' [45 *p. 106*]. On the basis of the White Paper, Wilson announced in the Commons that the government would be re-opening negotiations, but he emphasised that the government would be going into them with an open mind [*Doc. 9a*]. In the debate which followed, he taunted the Conservatives for appearing to be willing to sacrifice cheap food and other national interests without seeking any corresponding advantages. The same ambivalent approach figured in Labour pronouncements during the general election campaign of June 1970.

6 HEATH AND BRITISH ENTRY, 1970–74

'There was never any doubt', John Young has written, 'that Edward Heath would press for EEC membership with greater vigour than Wilson' [45 p. 107]. Sir Roy Denman, a member of the negotiating team appointed by Wilson, has gone further. In his view, 'had Wilson won the election, negotiations for entry would have failed and Britain would not now be a member of the European Union' [35 p. 231]. Unlike Wilson, Heath was fully committed to the idea of joining Europe. He had seen the terrible consequences of nationalism at first hand as an officer in the allied army liberating France and Belgium in 1944–45 and as an observer at the Nuremburg trials. He made his maiden speech in the House of Commons in June 1950 attacking Ernest Bevin for his policy on the Schuman plan. In 1961–63 he led the British negotiating team, and vowed, after de Gaulle's veto, that 'we in Britain' would not 'turn our backs on Europe' [108 p. 492]. His commitment to Europe can in part be explained by his relative lack of commitment to the other two 'circles' constraining British policy. Unlike his predecessors, up to and including Wilson, he was not a 'Commonwealth man', and he appears to have regarded the Commonwealth mainly as an irritant. He was also decidedly cool about the Anglo–American relationship. He disliked the term 'special relationship', and he urged that London should 'turn more to Paris, Bonn or Rome' [14 p. 241]. Anglo–American relations deteriorated considerably over the course of his premiership. His ambivalence towards America was not shared by the majority in his own party nor was the extent of his commitment to Europe. Nevertheless, the Conservative Party had by now emerged as 'the party of Europe' – partly through its own endeavours, and partly through Labour's taunts.

THE LUXEMBOURG NEGOTIATIONS

Strictly speaking, Britain did not have to make a third application to join the Communities. The second still lay 'on the table', and was re-activated by the Labour government after the Hague summit. It was the Labour government which arranged for the resumption of nego-tiations on 30 June, and which drafted the statement made on that occasion by Anthony Barber, Heath's first 'Mr. Europe'. (Barber be-came Chancellor at the end of July, and was replaced by Geoffrey Rippon.)

The negotiations were by no means as easy as might have been ex-pected. At the first ministerial meeting, Barber was forced to wait for five and a half hours after making his statement, before the Council of Ministers called him back to hear their reply. During that time he looked increasingly like 'a nervous accountant awaiting the arrival of the auditors' [35 *p. 233*]. The British press were outraged at the sup-posed discourtesy [144 *pp. 23–4*]. Such discourtesies necessarily punctuated the negotiations at frequent intervals, however, since all arrangements, amendments and compromises demanded by Britain and the other applicants (Denmark, Ireland and Norway) had to be debated and then countered by 'the Six' as a whole. In 1961–63 this had not been the case: the negotiations then had been conducted between 'the Six' represented separately and the applicants in full conference. De Gaulle had not been alone in thinking that this method increased the opportunities for applicants to exploit divisions between the existing members and in fearing that the whole web of compromises and agreements which had established the Communities would begin to unravel [138 *pp. 78–81*].

At the time of the first British application, Monnet had advised the British to join first and to sort out the problems afterwards. In certain areas it was found that this was indeed the best procedure, either be-cause the problems were relatively insignificant, or because their dimensions could not be assessed until after entry. Nevertheless, on major issues Heath could not follow Monnet's advice: with such a small majority in the House of Commons (smaller than the number of known Conservative anti-Europeans), he could not 'be seen to concede too much' [45 *p. 108*]. Fortunately, the Commonwealth problem had diminished significantly by 1971. Britain took only 12 per cent of Australia's exports, for instance, and of those only half would be affected by tariff changes. Nevertheless, there were still three problems: New Zealand lamb and dairy products (accounting for 80 to 85 per cent of total New Zealand exports), Caribbean cane sugar (competing with surplus French beet production) and arrange-ments for trade with the newly-independent ex-colonial states. EFTA was no longer a problem, as 'the Six' were prepared to offer wide-ranging free trade agreements. Agriculture was also regarded as less of a problem, in as much as Heath recognised that, 'however much we should like it, there is no evidence that the Community will change the CAP as such' [144 *p. 36*]. His hand was strengthened by a temporary rise in world food prices in the early 1970s, which meant that CAP funds were in some cases used to subsidise the consumer rather than the farmer.

The most difficult items of the negotiations arose from aspects of Community policies which had been agreed since 1961–63, and which had therefore not been at issue in the original negotiations: in particular, the Community budget, monetary union and fisheries. At the Hague in 1969, 'the Six' had agreed (at Pompidou's insistence) to fix the principles of the Community budget before entering negotiations with Britain and other would-be members. The government estimated that at the end of any transitional period Britain would have to contribute some 21.5 per cent of the Community's budget, compared with a share of GNP of some 15 to 16 per cent and a likely share of receipts of only 8 to 9 per cent. The figures were, of course, difficult to project, as they depended on Britain's likely rate of economic growth, the extent to which its trade re-oriented towards Europe, movements in world food prices and the share of the Community budget expended on non-CAP items. Nevertheless, British acceptance of existing arrangements would clearly have a significant effect on Britain's balance of payments and its industrial competitiveness. The problem of monetary union also derived in large part from the Hague summit of 1969. 'The Six' were now committed to linking their exchange rates as the first step towards full monetary union but the special position of sterling made it difficult for Britain to join in such moves. The French Finance Minister, Valéry Giscard d'Estaing, insisted that Britain should run down sterling balances held on behalf of other countries in London before joining the Communities. The British insisted that the position of sterling was not a matter for negotiation. Finally, the problem of fisheries was not of any great importance in terms of GDP, but in terms of the psyche of an island nation it was an obstacle of potentially decisive importance. 'The Six' had agreed on a Common Fisheries Policy on 30 June 1970 – literally hours after opening negotiations with the four applicants, whose territorial waters were estimated to contain two-thirds of the fish-stocks of an enlarged Community. Under the terms of the policy, these stocks would be open to fishermen of all Community countries on equal terms. British demands for a moratorium during which new arrangements could be negotiated were at first flatly refused [138, 144].

The negotiations were already proving difficult by the beginning of

1971, when the French began to harden their attitude, taking a firmer line on such issues as New Zealand butter and British budget contributions. Heath now began to warn that he 'would not be able to present for the approval of Parliament' terms which were not 'tolerable in the short term and clearly and visibly beneficial in the long term' [137 *pp. 355–6*]. It was in these circumstances that Heath travelled to Paris for twelve hours of talks with Pompidou, accompanied only by interpreters, on 20–21 May 1971. 'We didn't want a good meeting – we needed a very, very good meeting', one of Britain's negotiators later remarked [138 *p. 119*]. When asked what he expected from the meeting, Pompidou said: 'The crux of the matter is that there is a European conception or idea, and the question to be ascertained is whether the United Kingdom's conception is indeed European' [137 *p. 358*]. The meeting turned largely on this question, and Heath's success in persuading Pompidou of Britain's European commitment was not only the turning-point of the negotiations, but arguably Heath's greatest diplomatic triumph. It 'would be unreasonable now to believe that an agreement is not possible', Pompidou declared at a joint press conference after the meeting; 'I have confidence in the England of Mr. Heath' [142 *p. 121*, 140].

After the Heath-Pompidou summit, France's representatives adopted a far more accommodating attitude in the negotiations. Agreements were reached on New Zealand butter and Caribbean sugar which were acceptable to the New Zealand government and the Caribbean sugar producers. Britain was allowed a six-year transitional period for CAP and the common external tariff. On fisheries the outlines of an agreement were approved, whereby Britain was allowed to preserve 90 per cent of its fish catch for ten years, with a review to follow. The French now accepted British assurances that sterling balances would be gradually run down. The budgetary question still proved intractable, but Britain agreed to accept a phasing-in of contributions over seven years, together with an assurance that if problems became unacceptable 'the very survival of the Community would demand that the institutions find equitable solutions' [22 *p. 59*]. At the end of June, the Council of Ministers announced that agreement had been reached with Britain on all the major outstanding issues [138, 140, 144].

SELLING EUROPE IN BRITAIN

On the basis of the terms agreed in Luxembourg, the government drafted a White Paper recommending British entry. This was almost untrustworthily positive. There was 'no question of any erosion of essential national sovereignty'; moreover, the government was 'confident that membership of the enlarged Community' would bring 'much improved efficiency and productivity in British industry', leading to 'faster growth of real wages' and 'a higher rate of growth' [*Doc. 9b*]. The White Paper was published in July 1971. Perhaps wisely, Heath left it until the end of October 1971 to press through a Commons vote on the issue.

Public opinion had been broadly favourable to EEC membership at the time of the first and second applications, but from de Gaulle's second veto onwards support had fallen away. A poll conducted for the European Commission early in 1970 found that only 23 per cent of British respondents were in favour of joining the Community – compared with 88 per cent of respondents in 'the Six' who favoured British entry [23 *p. 131*]. Opinion polls showed British support for entry increasing thereafter but by the summer of 1971 the gap was still enormous. Some of the increase in support can be attributed to what Wilson referred to as a 'vast propaganda campaign' by the government; some to the activities of the European Movement, the Federal Trust and other well-funded pressure groups. Nevertheless, anti-market groups also sprang into action. The Keep Britain Out group had a particular knack for publicity stunts. More serious opposition came from the trade union movement, especially the Transport and General Workers' Union and the National Union of Mineworkers. On the other hand, only the *Express* newspapers opposed entry: even the *Daily Mirror* and the *Sun* (both at that time Labour supporters) favoured membership. Business, represented through the CBI, was strongly in favour [138].

Opposition to Heath's policies within the Conservative Party was relatively mute. Two possible leaders, Sir Alec Douglas-Home and Reginald Maudling, had already decided not to rock the boat. The only anti-market figure of any weight, Enoch Powell, was already confined to the hysterical fringe of the party and was widely reviled for his racist views. Nevertheless, there was evidence of a more broadly-based unease in the Conservative Party at grass-roots. Some 20 to 30 MPs, by no means all Powellites, were reckoned to be willing to vote against the government. The vote at the annual party conference in mid-October – 2474 to 324 in favour of entry on the negotiated terms – said more about Conservative Party loyalty than about the dimensions of support for membership. Against his own inclinations, Heath was persuaded by the Conservative Chief Whip, Francis Pym, to allow a free vote in the Commons. Pym calculated that a free vote would not greatly increase the number of Conservative dissenters, while it would make the Labour leadership's position far more difficult [137, 138].

The Labour Party was still deeply divided on the issue. 'As the Minister who began these negotiations', George Thomson declared, 'these are terms which I would have recommended a Labour cabinet to accept'. George Brown agreed. 'Challenging they may be, but they are fair', he said [142 *p. 156*]. Brown had lost his seat at the election and it was Roy Jenkins who emerged as the leader of the Labour pro-marketeers. The anti-marketeers comprised a slightly larger group, strengthened by TUC opposition and by an increase in the proportion of left-wingers in the parliamentary party after the 1970 election. Wilson at first hesitated. His mind appears to have been made up by Callaghan's decision to come out against entry in May 1971 (with a florid speech declaring EEC membership a threat to the English language). Wilson feared an attempt to oust him, by an unholy alliance of Callaghan, the left and the unions. Jenkins pleaded with him to 'take the hard, difficult, consistent, unpopular line', in the interests of his own 'long-term reputation', but without success. Wilson soon declared himself opposed to the terms on offer [40 *pp. 319–20*]. In July, a special Labour conference followed his lead, as did meetings of the National Executive Committee and the TUC. At the October annual conference, trade union votes helped to ensure a five-to-one majority against membership. Jenkins had already let it be known that he would vote for membership whatever the official line of the Labour Party. Over the summer the question was how many of his colleagues would follow him. One observer described the situation in the Labour Party as 'civil war' [40, 138].

The crucial Commons debate took place on 21 to 28 October 1971. The Labour parliamentary party had voted by 140 to 111 in favour of a three-line whip against entry. The debate had an air of unreality about it, since Jenkins and his colleagues were forced to sit through it in silence. Wilson attempted to portray the negotiated terms as 'intolerable', and played on public perceptions of the EEC as run by an out-of-touch bureaucracy handing out 'doles' to European farmers [*Doc. 9c*]. Picking up on an idea first put forward by Callaghan, he insisted that Labour would re-negotiate the terms of entry. But, asked what he would do if the re-negotiations failed, he replied merely, 'we would sit down amicably and discuss the situation' [8, 28 Oct. 1971, cols 2103–4]. Summing up for the government, Heath made a reasoned but not overly impressive case for entry, although he rose to the historic nature of the occasion by concluding that 'many millions of people right across the world' would 'rejoice' if Britain voted to enter [8, 28 Oct. 1971, col. 2212]. The result was a triumph for Heath, or, rather, for Pym and Jenkins: 356 to 244 in favour of entry. Thirty-nine Conservatives voted against, with two abstentions. On the Labour side, 68 MPs followed Jenkins into the 'Aye' lobby, and a further 20 abstained. The Liberals split five to one in favour of entry, while the Ulster Unionists voted solidly against. When the result was announced, Harold Macmillan lit an enormous bonfire waiting on the cliffs of Dover, which was answered by another waiting on the shores of France [137].

The parliamentary battle was by no means over. The Treaty of Accession was signed on 22 January 1972, Heath declaring that the ceremony marked both 'an end and a beginning' [*Doc. 9d*]. The Treaty necessitated the passage of a European Communities Bill. Jenkins and the majority of his colleagues were now forced to toe the Labour Party line, reasoning that it was up to Heath to find his own majority. The bill took up 300 hours of parliamentary time, and was put to 94 divisions. At one point the government majority fell to four, but there were always enough 'old men who had decided their political fate no longer mattered and young men with the gallantry of 1916 subalterns' to ensure sufficient Labour abstentions for the bill to pass into law [40 *p. 338*]. On 13 July 1972, the third reading was secured by a majority of seventeen, and on 17 October the bill received the royal assent. Referenda having been held in Denmark, Ireland, Norway and France – those in Denmark and Ireland approving entry, that in Norway rejecting it, and that in France approving the enlargement – Britain, Denmark and Ireland officially entered the European Communities on 1 January 1973.

BRITAIN IN EUROPE

As a number of writers have pointed out, Britain chose the worst moment at which to join the European Communities: just when the long economic boom of the 1950s and 1960s was coming to an end, to be replaced by much harder economic climes. Not only was Europe unable to offer that vast expansion of trade promised by the government White Paper but also the economic climate made it far more difficult for Britain to adjust to membership and allowed anti-marketeers to paint Britain's misfortunes as the result of EC membership. The weakness of the international economy had been prefigured in a series of monetary crises in the late 1960s. The slide into international recession was already underway by the time the OPEC oil-producing states doubled the price of oil in October 1972, and doubled it again in December 1973. For the rest of the decade, Britain and other western industrialised countries experienced low or negative economic growth, spiralling inflation, rising unemployment, and more frequent and bitter industrial conflict.

Britain had already begun participating in the work of the Communities before membership formally began. In October 1972, the leaders of the 'six plus three' met in Paris, and agreed a wide-ranging programme of work. Heath's advocacy can be seen in the agreement to create a European Regional Development Fund (ERDF)* – the aim of which was to channel EC money towards the development of depressed industrial areas. Britain could expect to receive a large proportion of this, off-setting the disadvantages of the CAP. Germany, which could expect to foot most of the bill, accepted the idea in return for a promise of progress on economic and monetary union. The Paris summit set a deadline for completion of the latter, 31 December 1980. The summit also agreed two further steps advocated by Britain: the formulation of a common energy policy and the development of a common EC stance ahead of the GATT trade talks scheduled for 1973. Heath was less happy with two other agreements, covering the formulation of common technological and industrial policies and the development of a common social policy (including trade union participation in management and harmonisation of social security schemes).

As David Reynolds has written, Heath's 'Europeanism was selective' [14 *p. 246*]. He pursued the ERDF proposal with vigour but refused to see it linked to progress on other issues. Germany's reluctance to contribute to a substantial fund was increased by this, as well as by the economic crisis. Meanwhile, France and other countries argued about the distribution of ERDF funds. At one point, the British negotiators threatened to veto progress on all other Community issues, unless agreement was reached on lines acceptable to Britain. Eventually the ERDF was set up in December 1974 but with much more limited resources than Heath had demanded or even expected. His enthusiasm in this area was in stark contrast to his attitude towards economic and monetary union. He flatly refused to put sterling into the joint float which was the first step towards monetary union. Britain did join the 'snake' which linked European exchange rates in May 1972 but pulled out the following month. Currency fluctuations ensured that this first attempt at monetary union ended in failure. Heath's awkwardness was again visibly illustrated in relation to plans for a common energy policy. He was originally one of the leading advocates of such a policy, which he envisaged as increasing the EC countries' bargaining power as oil consumers. However, he opposed a corresponding agreement on the distribution of energy resources within the EC. With North Sea oil beginning to be developed, the British press saw a plot to deprive Britain of its oil. Against the background of a miners' strike, power cuts and a state of emergency, Heath went to the Copenhagen summit in December 1973 determined to block any agreement on internal regulation. This he succeeded in doing.

Domestic pressure compelled Heath to appear tougher on the Europeans than perhaps he would have liked. Moreover, being 'European' did not rule out pursuing British national interests. National interests, after all, had been what brought Britain and the other EC countries together in the first place. Nevertheless, Heath showed himself un*communautaire* in the way he steadily blocked progress in areas important to other countries, while demanding special treatment in areas of particular interest to Britain. Heath compounded this by acting as if he knew better than other Europeans what was good for Europe, as in his persistent attempts to tinker with established Community institutions. By the time his government fell, in a bungled showdown with the miners in February 1974, Britain had already begun to acquire a reputation as an 'awkward partner' [36].

7 THE LABOUR GOVERNMENTS, 1974–79

In the general election held on 28 February 1974 Labour won four more seats than the Conservatives but fell a long way short of a Commons majority. The minor parties won 37 seats, the Liberals and Scottish Nationalists doing particularly well. Heath attempted to form a government, but failed. On 4 March Wilson became Prime Minister for the second time. A second election, on 10 October 1974, produced a Labour majority of three. Nevertheless, a series of by-election defeats meant that after November 1976 Labour was once more in a minority. From March 1977 the government clung to power by means of the 'Lib-Lab' pact and a precarious alliance with the Welsh and Scottish Nationalists. By this time Callaghan, Foreign Secretary in Wilson's government, had replaced Wilson as Prime Minister.

Edmund Dell, who served as a minister under both Wilson and Callaghan, has written that 'the Labour Government elected in 1974 faced the most difficult economic and political baptism of any postwar British administration except that of Attlee' [150, *p. vii*]. Partly because of the rise in oil prices, partly as a consequence of the credit boom unwisely introduced by the Conservative Chancellor, Anthony Barber, in 1972–73, the economic situation inherited by Labour was characterised by negative growth, rising unemployment, mounting inflation and an increasing balance of payments deficit. Denis Healey, Chancellor throughout 1974–79, attempted to deal with the situation by mobilising Labour's 'social contract' with the trade unions, which restricted wage inflation, and by international borrowing on a massive scale. He was reluctant to implement public expenditure cuts until the prolonged sterling crisis of March–December 1976 necessitated them, as part of the conditions for an IMF loan. Thereafter, Healey was successful in restraining public expenditure and public sector borrowing, and curbing inflation – which had peaked at 30 per cent in 1975. Nevertheless, this was at the price of still higher unemployment, the breakdown of the alliance with the trade unions, and the alienation of the Labour left. The 1978–79 'winter of discontent' heralded the collapse of Callaghan's government [152].

Both the government's precarious political position and the country's economic problems inevitably had an impact on Britain's relations with its European partners. The government's European policy was unusually susceptible to short-term domestic pressures, and while a more positive European policy was a condition of Liberal support, it was fiercely resisted by the majority of Labour left-wingers. Moreover, the case put for EEC membership in 1971 – that it would lead to a new era of economic growth – was proved wildly over-optimistic, and EEC membership was instead associated with higher prices and economic stagnation.

LABOUR AND EUROPE

The issue of EEC membership had been deeply divisive within the Labour Party at the time of Britain's entry. Nevertheless, the fact of British entry contributed to a lowering of the temperature. At the October 1972 party conference, the formula of renegotiation followed by a popular vote on the issue ensured that Wilson 'was now effectively committed to making faces at the Europeans, but not – critically – to a path of negotiations that might lead to withdrawal' [131 *p. 598*]. To many observers, Wilson's commitment to renegotiate was a sleight of hand. The Labour Party 'was deeply split between those strongly for continued membership of the Community despite the terms which Heath had negotiated, and those strongly against' [150 *p. 17*]. The terms achieved through any renegotiation were unlikely to make much impact on this division. Nevertheless, Wilson's strategy was a successful holding operation. With an election increasingly likely, Wilson was even able to welcome Jenkins back into the shadow cabinet (from which he had resigned in March 1972), in October 1973.

Labour's February 1974 manifesto declared that Heath's government had made 'a profound political mistake' by entering the EEC on the terms negotiated. Labour promised 'a fundamental renegotiation of the terms of entry', and in particular to seek 'major changes' in the CAP, 'new and fairer methods of financing the Community budget' and 'the retention by Parliament of those powers needed to pursue effective regional, industrial policies'. After the renegotiation, the people would be 'consulted' – whether by means of an election or a referendum not being, at this stage, made clear [147]. The manifesto pleased the left-wing opponents of the EEC, who increasingly dominated the trade unions, the constituency parties and the National Executive Committee, but it also kept the door open to the Jenkinsites, who deduced that a successful renegotiation would lead a Labour government to endorse membership. Wilson himself appears to have hoped to keep Britain in the Community. Callaghan was less convinced. His first major speech as Foreign Secretary criticised the Europeans for their supposed anti-Americanism. At one point 'he attacked a decision of the Community's Council of Ministers. He was reminded that he was now one of them. He retorted that he did not feel like one'. His hostility to Europe was 'slowly eroded by the advice of his officials' [35 *p. 247*]. Nevertheless, for Callaghan as well as for Wilson, 'joining the Common Market was like getting up on a Monday morning; it was something one might have to do, but it was not something to get excited about' [153 *p. 73*].

THE RENEGOTIATIONS

A charitable interpretation of Wilson's comings and goings over Europe portrays him as genuinely convinced of the merits of British membership, but equally convinced that only by negotiating better terms could his administration win over sufficient Labour activists and members of the general public to make British membership secure [131 *p. 636*, 132]. A more cynical interpretation portrays him as a scheming opportunist, mischievously opposing Heath for party political reasons in 1971, then manipulating the Labour Party and public opinion when confronted by the realities of power. At the time, Jenkins inclined towards this second interpretation. As he later noted, 'the whole exercise [of renegotiation] had more of cosmetics than of reality about it' [40 *p. 387*]. From the opposite side of the Labour divide, Barbara Castle also suspected that Wilson and Callaghan were merely seeking 'a patch-up deal to stay in' [*Doc. 10b*].

Callaghan, who had full control of the negotiations, embarked on them with a surprisingly conciliatory speech in the House of Commons on 19 March 1974, in which he emphasised that the government would 'not aim to conduct the negotiations as a confrontation', and that it would 'embark on these fundamental talks in good faith, not to destroy or to wreck but to adapt and reshape' [8, 19 March 1974, col. 865]. Pressure from the left wing in Cabinet ensured that Callaghan took a firmer line at the meeting of the Council of Ministers in Luxembourg at which he tabled Britain's demands. The government was 'engaged in a root and branch review. ... We are not asking for charity. We seek a fair deal' [*Doc. 10a*].

The Treaty of Accession made no provision for a renegotiation of the terms of entry, and Britain's European partners would have been within their rights to call Wilson's bluff by refusing one. This might well have happened had Pompidou still been French President; but Pompidou died early in April 1974, and was replaced by the more accommodating – though certainly no more Anglophile – Giscard d'Estaing. Helmut Schmidt, who replaced Brandt as German Chancellor soon after, was also willing to be helpful. Nevertheless, the Europeans were understandably irritated by the whole episode and by the British government's conduct. In November, Wilson made up a wholly false story of how he had fended off proposals to introduce a 'Euro-loaf' and 'Euro-beer', through the introduction of common purity standards. Schmidt, who aspired to the role of a world statesman, and in whose vision Europe figured largely, was outraged to learn that for Callaghan 'the touchstone' of the Community was 'what would please the British housewife' [30 *p. 236*].

Callaghan set out a number of demands, which formed the basis of the renegotiations. Some of them were entirely meaningless. The British government's right to exempt certain basic items from VAT, to limit capital movements between Britain and Europe, and to undertake measures of regional and industrial planning, had never been disputed. The EMU was a paper tiger now that France had left the fixed exchange-rate system, and there was never any question of forcing Britain in. The fact that negotiation on these points was a charade did not prevent Wilson and Callaghan making the most of their 'victories'.

On other, more substantial issues, Britain's partners were helpful, although not overly inclined to be seen to capitulate to British pressure. The demand for an extension of the Yaoundé agreement to Commonwealth and other developing countries tied in with a more general desire to improve Europe's relations with the 'third world'. The Lomé Convention* of February 1975, which guaranteed quotas and tariff exemptions for developing countries' exports, has been criticised as perpetuating the relationship of dependency and over-reliance on unprofitable commodities. At the time it was welcomed as generous; but it was by no means the result of purely British pressure [24]. Britain did succeed in getting an agreement to extend the special arrangements for sugar from Commonwealth countries but an agreement on New Zealand butter was more difficult to secure. Britain's demand for reform of the CAP was supported by Schmidt but virulently opposed by Giscard. A few very minor concessions were won but, in general, all that Britain was able to achieve was an agreement to review the bases of the pricing policy. The most difficult item in the negotiations was the size of Britain's budget contribution. In May 1974 the Treasury forecast that at the end of the transitional arrangements (in 1980) Britain would be contributing 24 per cent of the budget, compared with a share of GNP of only 14 per cent. Britain's grievance was recognised by some Community members, but not at first by France, which stuck rigidly to the doctrine that import levies (and even VAT contributions) were the Community's 'own resources', and therefore could not be described as 'British' contributions.

On the eve of the Dublin summit in March 1975 – the first of the regular summits described as meetings of the European Council* – two issues remained outstanding: New Zealand butter and the British budget contribution. Agreement on the latter appeared close, however, on the basis of a Commission formula awarding a rebate to any net contributor satisfying certain criteria (relating to its balance of payments, growth rate, share of GNP, etc.), the rebate to be two-thirds of the gap between its budget contribution and its share of GNP, but not more than the amount of its VAT contributions. Schmidt and Giscard hoped that the Dublin summit would be another milestone along the path of European integration but at Wilson's insistence it was dominated by Britain's unfinished business. Eventually, the Commission formula was agreed, but with the additional proviso that any rebate should be limited to 250 million units of account (roughly £125 million). The summit also agreed to extend the existing arrangements for New Zealand butter beyond 1977. Wilson portrayed the summit as a triumph, and himself as 'a "St George" figure, who knew how to stand up to foreign dragons and would never sell his country short' [36 *p. 86*]. That there was 'nothing of any value gained in the exercise which could not have been obtained in the continuous negotiation ... which is a fact of Community life' was not allowed to stand in his way. The result was 'the minimum of gain for the maximum of irritation' [35 *pp. 249–50*].

THE 1975 REFERENDUM

During the 1970 election campaign Heath had promised that British entry into the European Community would only take place 'with the full-hearted consent of Parliament and people' [45 *p. 108*]. This had always been a weak point in his case for membership which Wilson had fully exploited in the long-running battle over entry. The idea of a referendum was first put forward by opponents of membership. In opposition, Wilson had picked up on it as a means of avoiding a clear-cut decision. In office, he saw it as an opportunity to settle the question once and for all. The Jenkinsites initially opposed the idea, but soon came round to it, as opinion polls showed support for British membership once more picking up, and as it became clear that Wilson and Callaghan were manoeuvring towards support of continuing British membership. One question still remained: how to prevent the issue blowing Labour apart. On 21 January 1975 the Cabinet accepted Wilson's proposal to abandon collective responsibility. Two days later, Wilson announced the decision to the House of Commons. The government would recommend either to stay in or to leave the Community, but individual ministers would 'be free to support and speak in favour of a different conclusion in the referendum campaign'. Meanwhile, Jenkins and his supporters turned up the heat by declaring that they would resign if the Cabinet failed to produce a recommendation in favour of membership [40 *p. 400*].

The crucial Cabinet meeting took place on 17 and 18 March 1975 after Wilson had returned from Dublin. Wilson reckoned that when he had originally formed his Cabinet, there had been 'eight for Europe, ten against and five wobblies'. Now the Cabinet divided 16–7 in favour [145 *pp. 342–9*]. On 9 April the government put its recommendation to the Commons. The 396–172 majority disguised the deep divisions within the Labour Party. 137 Labour MPs voted in favour of the government's recommendation, but 145 (including 38 ministers) voted against, with 33 abstentions. The government was saved by the Conservative Party – now led by Margaret Thatcher, who had defeated Heath in a leadership challenge in February – which voted 249–8 in favour, with 18 abstentions. The referendum was set for 5 June, with the question, 'Do you think that the United Kingdom should stay in the European Community (the Common Market)?'.

The Cabinet and Commons decisions enabled the pro-marketeers to write the government's pamphlet, *Britain's New Deal in Europe*, which was delivered to every household in Britain [*Doc. 11a*]. Wilson and Callaghan played a relatively minor role in the campaign which followed, although both made last-minute interventions on the pro-market side. The leading Labour pro-marketeer was Jenkins, who also served as President of the all-party Britain in Europe campaign. Benn (who had by now changed sides) soon emerged as the leading Labour 'anti', his position as Secretary of State for Industry adding weight to his predictions of the dire consequences of membership for unemployment and state control of industry. Peter Shore was equally effective, although tending to concentrate on the more esoteric question of the threat to national sovereignty. The Labour movement as a whole swung firmly behind the 'No' vote. A special conference in April voted two-to-one against membership. In May, the TUC issued a broadsheet which was widely circulated, condemning membership as 'damaging to the economy, damaging to industry, and damaging to our democratic freedoms' [*Doc. 11b*].

The Conservative Party was far less divided on the issue than Labour. Heath, determined to prove himself still a political force to be reckoned with, sprung to life as the leading Conservative spokesman for the cause of membership. His successor as leader took a secondary role, although she made clear her support for the 'Yes' campaign. In an article for the *Daily Telegraph* on the eve of the poll, she reiterated the arguments for membership, putting at the top of her list 'the peace and security of Europe' [*Doc. 11c*]. Conservative 'antis' were noticeable mostly by their insignificance. Powell was ubiquitous, but had fatally undermined his influence with grass-roots Conservatives by openly supporting Labour in the February 1974 election (solely on the European issue), then joining the Ulster Unionists. The only other Conservative 'anti' of any weight was Neil Marten.

Most of the campaigning was conducted under the auspices of pressure groups, and in particular the two 'umbrella' groups set up to channel government funds and write the other two pamphlets which were distributed to every house in Britain. The contrast between them was striking. Britain in Europe was a smooth publicity machine, with excellent contacts in business, the press and the academic world. It encompassed leading moderates from all the main parties, as well as such figures as Vic Feather (former general secretary of the TUC) and Sir Henry Plumb (leader of the National Farmers' Union). Above all, it was well funded, raising more than £1.3 million in addition to the £125,000 received from public funds. The National Referendum Campaign, the main 'anti' group, raised an additional £6,354. What it lacked in funds it made up for in enthusiasm. However, this merely increased its inability to persuade the general public. The sight of Benn and Powell sharing a platform supported by the Communist Party and the National Front merely confirmed the truism that 'extremes meet' [146, 153].

The result of the referendum was never in doubt. From the moment it was announced, opinion polls showed a two-to-one lead for the 'Yes' campaign. 64.5 per cent of the electorate voted (not far short of a general election turnout). 17,378,581 cast a 'Yes' vote, 8,470,073 a 'No'. The Shetland and the Western Isles voted 'No', but otherwise every county or region recorded a majority for membership – even

Northern Ireland, where the Unionists campaigned against [*Doc. 11d*]. 'Fourteen years of national argument are over', Wilson declared. 'It is really thrilling', Mrs Thatcher reportedly affirmed [131 *p. 660*]. For Wilson, it was in a very real sense a victory. 'In all my thirteen years as Leader of the Party I had no more difficult task than keeping the Party together on this issue', he later admitted [155 *p. 51*]. At the time, there had been much talk of a repeat of 1931, when a previous Labour leader (Ramsay MacDonald) had broken with the majority of his party to lead a Tory-dominated coalition in order to safeguard what he perceived as the national interest. That this had not happened was, in Ben Pimlott's view, 'one of Wilson's most remarkable achievements, perhaps the greatest triumph of his career' [131 *p. 654*].

In the politically charged atmosphere of the 1980s and 1990s, British opponents of Europe frequently asserted that the public had been 'hoodwinked' in 1975: in particular, that the fundamental issue of national sovereignty had not been addressed, and had in fact been concealed from the voters [137 *p. 686*, 31]. There is some truth in this. The renegotiations succeeded admirably in strengthening politicians' propensity to focus on bread-and-butter issues, and much of the argument revolved around economic costs and benefits. The pro-Europeans did tend to play down the long-term political implications. Nevertheless, these were raised by anti-marketeers, notably Shore and Powell, and were addressed by their opponents. In the Commons debate in April, Heath echoed Churchill's message of 1948: 'sovereignty is not something to be hoarded, sterile and barren. ... Sovereignty is something for us as custodians to use in the interests of our country' [137 *p. 685*]. Heath's enthusiasm for Europe was, of course, unique. David Butler and Uwe Kitzinger found little such enthusiasm in the country: 'The referendum was not a vote cast for new departures or bold initiatives. ... The verdict was not even necessarily a vote of confidence that things would be better in than out; it may have been no more than an expression of fear that things would be worse out than in' [146 *p. 280*].

AN AWKWARD PARTNER?

George Thomson, now an EC Commissioner, warned in 1975 that Britain had 'substantially run down our working capital of goodwill' in the Community, as a result of the antics over renegotiation and the referendum [10 *p. 253*]. The Europeans had been prepared to be tolerant and even helpful while Wilson could claim to be ploughing a furrow for Europe. With the referendum over, it was time to get down to business. In Britain, however, the referendum appears to have been less of a milestone than a hurdle, and attitudes changed little. The Labour anti-marketeers regrouped as the Common Market Safeguards Committee. Opinion polls consistently showed attitudes towards EC membership evenly balanced after 1975. Averaged out, eighteen polls taken over the period 1974–82 found that 33 per cent of British respondents thought membership of the EC a 'good thing', 23 per cent thought it 'neither good nor bad', and 37 per cent thought it a 'bad thing'. The equivalent figures for France were 57 per cent, 28 per cent and 7 per cent [30 *p. 235*].

Public opinion may explain why Britain was a reluctant partner in the Community; that it was an awkward partner was largely the work of the government. The French had been given a foretaste of this in January 1975 when the British government abruptly cancelled a Channel Tunnel project – after the French had already dug a large hole in the *Pas de Calais*. Similar insensitivity bedevilled relations between Britain and the Community as a whole. In July 1975 the attempt to build a common environmental policy was almost derailed when Britain insisted on exceptions from emission limits designed to curb the pollution of rivers. In December, Britain was again in a minority of one on the issue of representation at the Conference on International Economic Co-operation. Britain's partners agreed on common representation, but Wilson demanded to be represented separately because of Britain's status as a prospective oil producer. Eventually Wilson was forced to climb down. In the first half of 1977 Britain held the presidency of the EC – meaning that British ministers chaired meetings of the Council of Ministers, Britain hosted the European Council, and the government bore responsibility for maintaining the Community's impetus and direction. The presidency was noted for two disputes, in which Britain was isolated: the first concerning the allocation of fish quotas following the general declaration of 200–mile fishing limits, the second concerning the agricultural price review, which John Silkin held up for a month (to the great inconvenience of farmers) for the sake of 1½ pence a lb. on the butter subsidy. One Labour supporter observed that ministers gave the impression of believing that the British presidency 'represented a *carte blanche* for Britain to get her own way for six months' [35 *pp. 255–7*, 36 *pp. 121–4*].

Schmidt and Giscard were determined to press ahead with integration. Two projects in particular emerged: direct elections to the European Parliament, and a revival of monetary union. In both cases

Britain was again awkward to the point of being obstructive. Direct elections figured in the Treaties of Rome, and were a longstanding demand of the European federalists. Only direct elections, they argued, could produce a Parliament sufficiently effective, representative and European-minded to act as a democratic check on the growing European bureaucracy. Callaghan reluctantly agreed to the principle in September 1976, but the following month the Labour Party condemned the idea at its annual conference. Callaghan did nothing, until the terms of the Lib-Lab pact committed him to pushing through the necessary legislation. Further delays meant that the elections right across Europe had to be postponed until Britain was at last ready, in June 1979 [36 *pp. 117–21*]. The question of a European Monetary System (EMS)* was raised by Roy Jenkins, who had left British politics to become President of the European Commission at the start of 1977. For different reasons, it was enthusiastically endorsed by Giscard and Schmidt. Healey believed that the EMS would only serve German interests, and he thought that currency stabilisation was best achieved through the IMF [151 *p. 439*]. Within the Labour Party more generally, there was considerable opposition on the grounds of national sovereignty. In July 1978 the Europeans pressed forward, with an agreement to start an Exchange Rate Mechanism (ERM),* a European Monetary Fund, and a new unit of account, the European Currency Unit (ecu),* based on a 'basket' of national currencies. Britain joined the EMS, by virtue of signing the agreement, but declined to join the ERM. Only in October 1990 did it do so. Meanwhile, Britain's position was conspicuous. As Sean Greenwood has noted, membership of the ERM 'was viewed as an indicator of a certain European *esprit de corps*' [38 *p. 106*].

Towards the end of Callaghan's administration, another row was brewing, in the form of the budget question. In 1977–78 Britain's net contribution, manageable before 1975, reached the alarming figure of £540 million and rising [*Doc. 12b*]. The corrective mechanism agreed in 1975 failed to work, because not all the criteria were fulfilled. In November 1978 Callaghan announced that he would be seeking negotiations to resolve the issue, and in his budget speech the following April, Healey blamed Britain's EC contributions for diminishing what would otherwise have been a spectacular balance of payments surplus. The gloves were coming off for what would undoubtedly be a bruising argument [36 *pp. 131–4*].

8   THE THATCHER GOVERNMENTS, 1979–90

The May 1979 election ushered in eighteen years of Conservative rule, for eleven and a half of which Margaret Thatcher was Prime Minister. This twentieth-century record was achieved with a significantly smaller share of the vote than had taken the Conservatives to victory in any previous election – the reason being the scale of support for the centre parties. In June 1983 the Conservative vote actually fell from 44 to 42 per cent, but Thatcher was able to increase her Commons majority from 43 to 144. In June 1987 the Conservatives' share of the vote increased to 43 per cent but their majority was reduced to 102. The peculiarities of the British electoral system thus ensured that Thatcher was free of the immediate problems of party management which had plagued the two previous prime ministers. From this basis she was able to impress her own style on government and to launch what many observers have described as a revolution in British domestic policy.

The nature and extent of Thatcher's agenda were clear before 1979, although the implementation of her policies was necessarily gradual and uneven. In economic terms she was a 'monetarist', who saw control of the money supply as the key to low inflation, which in turn was the key to sustained economic growth. A staunch believer in free market principles, she aimed to reverse the corporatist and interventionist consensus which had animated British economic policy since 1945. This involved 'privatising' the nationalised industries, diminishing the power of the trade unions, restraining public expenditure, cutting taxes, removing obstacles to free enterprise, and attempting to widen the basis of property- and share-ownership. In Andrew Gamble's words, she 'sought to re-establish the conditions for making the Conservative Party the leading force once again in the British state' [160 *p. xi*, 162].

Thatcher's uncompromising style expressed itself in foreign as well as in domestic policy. Revelling in her nickname 'the Iron Lady', she aimed to 'make Britain great again' through a forceful assertion of national interests – as, most strikingly, in the Falklands war of 1982. Nevertheless, as David Reynolds has pointed out, 'rhetoric is not the same as reality'. Thatcher's approach to the rather more significant post-imperial problems of Rhodesia, Hong Kong and Northern Ireland was pragmatic and realistic, and in other areas her premiership 'was a case study in the possibilities and limitations of the diplomacy of bluff' [14 *pp. 256–7*]. The hallmark of her foreign policy was Atlanticism, strengthened after 1980 by the personal bond between herself and President Reagan. Thatcher's support for American policy underlined Britain's continuing commitment to the Anglo–American relationship. There was no Thatcherite 'revolution' in foreign policy. Indeed, Thatcher has been criticised precisely for failing to re-assess Britain's policies in the light of rapidly changing circumstances. Thatcher's Britain was thus increasingly 'marginalized' on the international scene [14 *p. 257*].

THE PARTY OF EUROPE

Sir Roy Denman has observed that in foreign policy Thatcher 're-mained the Grantham schoolgirl of the early wartime years. The Germans she detested. ... The French she despised. ... The Americans, our gallant allies, she adored' [35 *p. 259*]. Thatcher's instinctive anti-Europeanism certainly became clear in the last years of her premiership. Nevertheless, the earlier years were characterised by a less hostile approach. Significantly, she made no attempt to win the support of anti-Europeans in her leadership challenge to Heath, and as leader of the opposition she appeared conscious of the Conservatives' identity as the 'party of Europe'. At this stage, anti-Europeanism was still largely a Labour phenomenom, while the Conservative Party contained numerous pro-Europeans, including rising stars such as Michael Heseltine and Douglas Hurd as well as figures from the Heathite past such as Lord Carrington and Francis Pym, Thatcher's first two foreign secretaries. Europe was one of those rare issues on which many of Thatcher's colleagues felt both strongly and strong enough to oppose her, as she found out on a number of occasions. Prudence alone would therefore seem to have compelled her to keep her anti-Europeanism under wraps.

Nevertheless, it could also be argued that Thatcher's position on Europe itself changed and that the relatively benign approach of the early years was genuine. Thatcher had her own vision of the Communities, as a zone of prosperity and freedom compatible with Atlanticism and with other British interests. She frequently argued that the EC performed an essential function by uniting a substantial part of 'free' Europe against the Soviet menace. Ironically, she was determined that Britain should play a central part in developing co-operation in such fields as foreign policy. In economic terms, she argued that it was 'wholly in the interests of this country to be in, and remain in, the EEC'. Membership brought access to an enormous and prosperous market, encouraged inward investment, and enabled Britain to negotiate as part of the world's largest trading bloc [8, 29 April 1980]. Indeed, Thatcher hoped that the 'free market' aspects of the Community would be strengthened. On taking office, she saw 'no contradiction between a vigorous and effective membership of the European Community and vigorous and effective pursuit of Britain's interests' [8, 15 May 1979]. Only gradually did she come to see a contradiction. This was in large part in reaction to developments in the Community itself, which threatened to steer Europe away from the lines which Thatcher favoured.

LABOUR, LIBERALS AND SOCIAL DEMOCRATS

The Conservatives' reputation as the 'party of Europe' was strengthened by the adversarial nature of British politics, which pitted Thatcher's first administration against a Labour Party which was now firmly anti-European in policy and approach. This reflected a more general Labour drift to the left after 1979, symbolised by the election of Michael Foot as leader of the party in November 1980 and by the prominence of proposals for nationalisation and unilateral disarmament in the party's commitments. A special Labour conference at Wembley in January 1981 saw the triumph of the anti-market wing of the party. The Labour Party thus fought the election committed to withdraw from the EC 'well within the lifetime of the parliament' [Doc. 17a].

The Wembley conference appears to have been the last straw for many on the right of the Labour Party, who now responded to Roy Jenkins's call for a 'realignment of British politics'. With David Owen, Shirley Williams and Bill Rodgers, Jenkins launched the Social Democratic Party, which immediately formed an alliance with the Liberal Party, and achieved a series of remarkable successes in by-elections. In the June 1983 election, the 'Alliance' gained 7.8 million votes, 25 per cent of the total cast. Labour received just 8.5 million, or 28 per cent, its lowest share since 1918. Nevertheless, Labour retained 209 seats, whereas the Alliance won only 23. The chief beneficiary of the switch from Labour to the Alliance was, ironically, Thatcher.

The Alliance aimed to 'break the mould' of British politics. Although it continued to make spectacular gains in local government, the 1983 election was the high point of its national success. In the 1987 election it won a respectable 23 per cent of the votes, but only returned 22 MPs. In March 1988 the two parties merged as the Social and Liberal Democrats (after October 1989 the Liberal Democrats), although a small rump under David Owen continued as independent Social Democrats until 1990. Only in 1997 were the Liberal Democrats able to make a breakthrough in terms of parliamentary representation, by picking up votes from disenchanted Conservatives rather than from former Labour supporters.

Arguably, the major long-term significance of the 1983 election was its effect on the Labour Party, which in the eyes even of many committed socialists had performed so disastrously because it had made itself 'unelectable'. In October 1983, Neil Kinnock replaced Foot as leader, and began a long and arduous process of modernisation and policy review which was to culminate in the election of Tony Blair as Prime Minister in 1997. Labour's commitment to withdraw from Europe was ditched by the time of the 1987 election, and replaced by a promise to 'work constructively' in Europe [*Doc. 17b*]. The emergence of proposals for a 'social Europe' (including the protection of employment, trade union and welfare rights) ensured that by the time of the 1992 election Labour appeared considerably more committed to Europe than the Conservatives [*Doc. 17c*].

THE BRITISH BUDGET QUESTION

When Thatcher took office, it would have been reasonable to expect a more positive approach to Europe than from the previous government. However, this would have been to count without the British Budget Question, and Thatcher's determination to make of it a symbol of her defence of national interests. As a result, the BBQ (or Bloody British Question, as it was irreverently described in Brussels) came to dominate Britain's relations with its European partners for the next five years. The problem arose from the malfunctioning of the 1975 rebate mechanism and the escalating costs of the CAP. The sums involved were certainly large enough to cause concern, although not as large as was sometimes suggested: the deficit of £1 billion projected for 1979–80 amounted to little over 1 per cent of total government expenditure, or one-tenth of the British defence budget. Nevertheless, the very principle of the deficit offended Thatcher. Moreover, two very useful purposes would be served by a fight on the issue: softening the impact of public expenditure cuts at home, and projecting Thatcher's image as a slayer of foreign foes.

Thatcher opened her campaign at the Strasbourg European Council in June 1979, but it was only at the Dublin Council in November, when the Commission presented its proposals, that the argument got into full swing. The Commission proposed a rebate of £350 million and increased expenditure in Britain; Thatcher demanded the full £1 billion. There followed ten hours of acrimonious debate. Thatcher brushed aside the theory of 'own resources' with the assertion, 'It's my money I want back'. Meanwhile, all other Community business was held up, and the meeting broke up without agreement [*Doc. 12a*]. In April Thatcher rejected a much improved offer, but the following month Lord Carrington secured further improvements after a marathon 24-hour negotiating session. Thatcher was still inclined to reject the terms – which offered Britain roughly £800 million a year for 1980 and 1981, with the promise of a permanent settlement later – but Carrington and others threatened to resign unless she accepted. Reluctantly, Thatcher agreed the settlement at the Venice Council in June [165 *pp. 188–90*].

The settlement negotiated by Carrington was only temporary. Thatcher continued to press for a permanent settlement at every available opportunity. Her hand was strengthened by worries among other potential net contributors, especially after the accession of Greece in 1981 and in the light of negotiations for the membership of Spain and Portugal; and also by the fact that British consent was needed before EC revenue could increase beyond the 1 per cent VAT 'ceiling'. At one point Britain attempted to veto agricultural price levels in the Community and at another blocked an extra payment to the Community to cover an overspend on CAP. France, Italy and the European Parliament in turn delayed payment of the refunds already promised to Britain. More worryingly, President Mitterrand of France (who succeeded Giscard in 1981) talked openly of the possibility of a 'two-speed' Europe, with Britain accepting some 'special status' outside the inner core [36 *p. 150*]. As John Young has noted, this raised the spectre of putting Britain back where it was 'before 1973, sidelined in Europe, without direct influence on the Continentals' [45 *p. 147*].

Eventually an agreement was reached at Fontainebleau in June 1984, by which Thatcher accepted a rebate of 66 per cent of the difference between British VAT contributions (but not tariffs or import levies) and EC receipts. In return, she agreed an increase in EC revenue from 1 to 1.4 per cent of national VAT receipts. This agreement was little different from proposals rejected by Thatcher on several previous occasions [36 *p. 156*]. Even this did not end the matter, as the whole question was re-opened in 1987–88 as a result of an EC budget crisis and a decision to alter the basis of EC funding. In June 1987 Thatcher left the Foreign Secretary Sir Geoffrey Howe 'shaking with anger' after rejecting a solution agreed by the other EC leaders. Again she accepted, in February 1988, a solution which was very little different [36 *pp. 189–90*]. Thatcher's initial attitude was perhaps in this instance justified: as a result of the changes, net British contributions rose above £2 billion in 1989–90, even after taking into account the negotiated refund [*Doc. 12b*].

At the time, Thatcher argued that she was acting in the best interests of the Community by attempting to resolve the budget question: otherwise, British resentment would fester and prevent any constructive engagement with its partners. The domestic presentation of her policy gave a different impression, however. It was useful to Thatcher to play up British anti-Europeanism, and to portray her partners' concessions as the result of her own persistence. Like Wilson, she clothed herself in the robes of St George. Many observers have argued that her negotiating style was counter-productive: by raising the stakes, she forced other leaders to resist her [45 *p. 150*]. The longer-term effects were certainly unfortunate. The continentals became convinced that Britain were not 'in the company of a true "European"' [165 *p. 188*]. Thatcher, on the other hand, was 'persuaded ... that it always paid to be bloody-minded in dealings with the Community' [163 *p. 111*].

TOWARDS THE SINGLE MARKET

With the budget question for the moment settled, 'there were indications that, under Thatcher, Britain might be becoming more *communautaire*' [38 *p. 11*]. This was certainly the case in relation to the proposal to complete the single market, set out in a British government document, *Europe – The Future*, presented to the Fontainebleau Council in June 1984. As David Reynolds has pointed out, Thatcher's decision 'to play Euro-politics' was a direct response to the danger that Britain would be left on the sidelines in a 'two-speed' Europe [14 *p. 267*]. Nevertheless, the extent of Thatcher's commitment to the single market should not be underestimated. A common market in services as well as goods, the removal of 'non-tariff' barriers, and the free movement of capital and labour all figured in the original Treaties of Rome; they fitted in perfectly with Thatcher's commitment to deregulation and increasing opportunities for enterprise; and they promised rich pickings for British firms operating in such businesses as transport and financial services [*Doc. 13*]. Thatcher realised that she 'would have to seek alliances with other governments, accept compromises and use language which I did not find attractive' in order to attain her objective, but she thought the price worthwhile [164 *p. 548*].

Europe – The Future set out only in very general terms the aim of completing the single market. Lord Cockfield, Thatcher's nominee as European Commissioner, was entrusted with the task of drawing up a detailed plan. This he did in time for the Milan Council in June 1985, producing a list of almost 300 items of legislation necessary to achieve the objective, with a projected timetable for each. Unfortunately for Thatcher, Cockfield had 'gone native' during his brief time in Brussels, and he included in his programme such items as harmonisation of indirect taxation and the abolition of frontier controls, which were unacceptable to her. An even greater problem was that her European partners insisted on the need for far-reaching institutional change to accompany the single market. Thatcher realised that an extension of majority voting in the Council of Ministers would be necessary to carry out the programme, but she hoped to keep change to the minimum necessary to ensure success [*Doc. 13*]. At Milan, she was outvoted, and the Community proceeded to call an Intergovernmental Conference (IGC)* to examine further change. The principle of a single market was, however, agreed, and a deadline set for 1992.*

Further negotiation resulted in the 'Single European Act' (SEA),* agreed at the Luxembourg Council in December 1985 and ratified by the national parliaments soon thereafter. Thatcher portrayed this as a triumph for her diplomacy. The single market was to be achieved by 1992. Majority voting would be introduced in specific areas (thus ending the 'Luxembourg compromise'), but not on such matters as taxation, frontier controls and employment law. Moreover, most majority voting would be by so-called 'qualified' majority – i.e., roughly two-thirds of the votes in the Council of Ministers, crudely weighted in proportion to population [18 *pp. 252–3*]. On the other hand, Thatcher was forced to accept a commitment to move towards economic and monetary union. Moreover, on the question of institutional reform, Thatcher did not appear to realise 'the extent to which her acceptance of the Single Act brought her along the conveyor belt to closer union' [35 *p. 264*]. Thatcher's refusal to agree to the harmonisation of indirect taxation continued to cause dissension within the Community, while her refusal to remove frontier controls resulted in the inner core of Europe going ahead without her, by means of the Schengen agreement. Meanwhile, Cockfield was removed at the earliest opportunity, in 1988, by being denied the usual second term of office [158].

THE REVIVAL OF EUROPEAN INTEGRATION

Stephen George has emphasised the extent to which the single market programme was a response to the revival of the movement towards European integration, and an attempt to 'guide it in the British direction' [36 *p. 153*]. Such an attempt was perhaps long overdue. The goal of an 'ever closer union' was, of course, written into the Treaties of Rome; but the history of the Community showed that progress towards the goal was achieved in fits and starts, rather than by any smooth progression [22]. The mid- to late 1970s were a particularly fallow period for the Community, although the initiation of direct elections to the European Parliament gave the European movement cause for celebration. Altiero Spinelli, the veteran Italian federalist, was amongst those who entered the Parliament in 1979 determined to reform the European institutions. Partly through his efforts, the Parliament issued a Draft Treaty on European Union in February 1984 [157]. Meanwhile, other, more powerful, voices had joined in the call for reform of the European institutions. In November 1981, the foreign ministers of Germany and Italy produced the 'Genscher–Colombo plan' for a 'political union' of the EC countries [6 *p. 178*]. At Stuttgart in June 1983, Mitterrand and Helmut Kohl (who had succeeded Schmidt in October 1982) pushed through a 'Solemn Declaration' on European Union, and a commitment to 'relaunch' the movement towards unity. Thereafter, the Franco–German axis was again to prove the dynamo of Community integration.

Thatcher's response to these developments was unequivocally hostile. 'I do not believe in a federal Europe', she declared, 'and I think to ever compare it with the United States of America is absolutely ridiculous' [165 *p. 385*]. She was implacably opposed to any extension of the powers of the Commission or the 'European Assembly' (as she insisted on still calling the Parliament). Nevertheless, in a trade-off for the budgetary settlement and the single market agreement, she was forced at Fontainebleau in June 1984 to accept the appointment of a committee under James Dooge to enquire into the question of institutional reform. The majority reported in March 1985 strongly in favour of the extension of majority voting and an increase in the powers of the Commission and the European Parliament. At Milan in

June 1985, Thatcher accepted an extension of majority voting, and was forced to accept an IGC to look into further reform. The recommendations of the IGC were embodied in the Single European Act agreed in December 1985.

Stephen George has argued that the Single European Act set Europe 'on a course very similar to that desired by Britain'; indeed, it involved Britain 'in gaining more than it conceded' [36 *pp. 185, 206*]. On the other hand, Sean Greenwood has asserted that it 'tipped the scales emphatically in favour of the argument for new European institutions ... which, in turn, implied a further erosion of national sovereignty' [38 *p. 114*]. Amongst the policies introduced by the Act were economic and social cohesion, monetary union, and the development of common social and environmental policies. Moreover, the Act introduced a number of important institutional changes: the abandonment of the national veto on many issues, a new 'co-operation' procedure giving greater power to the European Parliament, and the formalisation of intergovernmental cooperation in foreign policy. As John Pinder has observed, rather than marking the limits of integration, as Thatcher hoped, the Single European Act contributed to the momentum for further change, by 'opening out new opportunities for the proponents of Union' [22 *p. 78*].

Thatcher came to regret signing the Single European Act, although she always believed that the problem was not so much with the Act itself as with its implementation. For this, she came increasingly to blame Jacques Delors, Commission President from January 1985. Surprisingly, Thatcher had endorsed Delors' candidacy, because he had been 'credited with reining back the initial left-wing socialist policies of President Mitterrand's Government' [164 *p. 547*]. Even more surprisingly, Thatcher endorsed Delors for a second term, largely on the grounds that the rival candidate was a German, and the Germans already held too many of the top jobs in international organisations [165 *p. 548*]. This was another decision she came to regret. Within days of the announcement of his second term, Delors boasted to the European Parliament that 'in ten years, 80 per cent of economic legislation – and perhaps tax and social legislation – will be directed from the Community' [36 *p. 193*]. In September 1988 he further enraged Thatcher by addressing her arch-enemies in the TUC, asserting that it was 'impossible' to conceive of a single market without a common social policy – a position which Thatcher had always rejected. Thatcher's response came in a speech at the College of Europe in Bruges. While careful to affirm that Britain's 'destiny is in Europe, as part of the Community', she went on to mount a thinly-veiled attack on Delors and on the whole movement towards European integration. 'We have not successfully rolled back the frontiers of the state in Britain, only to see them reimposed at a European level', she declared [*Doc. 14*].

The Bruges speech brought forth an enthusiastic response from sections of the British media and a growing number of 'Eurosceptics' within the Conservative Party. It also marked a turning-point in Thatcher's personal fortunes, in that it alienated a number of her senior and more moderate colleagues. Howe was 'deeply dismayed' by the speech, whose effect 'was to misunderstand or misrepresent the Community as it already existed and to inhibit its future in defiance of the texts that we had ourselves negotiated' [161 *p. 537*]. Howe also believed that Thatcher misjudged the popular mood – a belief confirmed by the results of the June 1989 European elections, when the Conservatives, campaigning against a 'diet of Brussels', for the first time won fewer seats than Labour [*Doc. 19*]. Howe and other moderates were further dismayed by the relish with which Thatcher now seemed to enjoy finding herself in a minority of one in Europe, as at Strasbourg in December 1989 on the question of a 'social charter', or again at Rome in October 1990, in relation to monetary union and a further IGC on political union.

BRITAIN AND THE ERM

Soon after taking office in 1979, the Conservatives announced that Britain would contribute towards the EMS monetary fund immediately and join the Exchange Rate Mechanism 'when the time was right'. It soon became clear, however, that Thatcher was opposed to joining the ERM on almost any terms. In her view, sterling was in an altogether different position from the other European currencies, because Britain was an oil exporter, and because sterling was far more vulnerable to fluctuations in the dollar than other European currencies. Moreover, she believed that membership would severely limit the government's freedom of action in economic policy, and would lead to high interest rates, enforced reductions in public expenditure, and higher unemployment. Full monetary union she was even less keen on, believing that it meant 'the end of a country's economic independence and thus the increasing irrelevance of its parliamentary democracy' [164 *p. 691*].

Nigel Lawson, Chancellor from 1983 to 1989, was a persistent advocate of joining the ERM, being convinced that it would provide the necessary discipline to bring down inflation. In 1985 he was joined by Howe. With support from a majority of their colleagues, the two ministers attempted to persuade Thatcher to approve ERM membership, but to little avail. There thus passed what Lawson later described as another 'missed opportunity' for Britain [163 *p. 501*]. Lawson then attempted to do the next best thing, which was to 'shadow' the value of the mark, as if Britain were already a member of the ERM. Nevertheless, Thatcher scuppered even this policy, by announcing that the fight against inflation was incompatible with 'excessive intervention' to support the pound, thus triggering a rise in the value of sterling beyond the ERM margin [36 *p. 191*].

The idea that monetary union was the essential corollary to completion of the single market was widely accepted on the continent. In June 1988 Kohl and Mitterrand decided that they could no longer allow Thatcher to obstruct progress, and pushed through a proposal for a committee under Delors to examine ways of moving towards a single currency managed by a central bank. Thatcher was again sidelined, protesting that 'I neither want nor expect to see such a bank in my lifetime, nor, if I'm twanging a harp, for quite a long time afterwards' [36 *p. 192*]. The Delors committee reported in April 1989, recommending a three-stage approach from currency alignment to the creation of a single currency. Meanwhile, Lawson and Howe succeeded in extracting a more positive approach to the ERM, by threatening to resign. At the Madrid Council in June 1989, Thatcher again made clear her opposition to a single currency, but she surprised many observers by her more co-operative stance on ERM [36 *pp. 216–18*]. She apparently intended this stance to be short-lived: the following month, she humiliatingly demoted Howe, and in October she provoked Lawson's resignation. Nevertheless, their two successors, Douglas Hurd and John Major, at last forced Thatcher to concede the inevitable and join the ERM in October 1990. Most observers are agreed that Britain chose the wrong exchange rate at which to join the ERM, and possibly the worst time to do so as well – just as German unification was pushing up interest rates, the dollar was beginning to slide, and Britain was entering the early stages of a recession. By now, also, it was too late for British entry to act as a restraining influence on moves towards further integration.

EUROPE AND THATCHER'S DOWNFALL

During her last years as Prime Minister, Thatcher was increasingly prone to outbursts of anti-Europeanism. Thus during a banquet supposedly to celebrate 40 years of Anglo–German friendship, she told a former German ambassador, 'You need another forty years before we can forget what you have done' [*35 p. 259*]. Thatcher's xenophobia became a political issue when one of her closest allies, Nicholas Ridley, gave an interview describing EMU as 'a German racket', and handing over power to the Community as the equivalent of 'giv[ing] it to Adolf Hitler'. Thatcher bowed to public pressure by sacking Ridley, but Lawson later confirmed what many believed at the time – that 'the reason why Nick Ridley felt it was safe' to make those remarks 'was that he had many times heard Margaret utter precisely the same sentiments in private' [*163 p. 900*]. Thatcher's shift towards hostility to Europe came at exactly the same time that British public opinion appeared to be shifting decisively in the opposite direction [*38 pp. 117–18*]. Moreover, it came at a time when changes in the international scene convinced many moderate Conservatives that a more constructive approach to Europe was needed. In particular, the end of the Cold War and the reunification of Germany underlined the necessity of tying Germany more firmly into European institutions. In such circumstances, Thatcher's prejudices seemed not only out of place, but distinctly dangerous.

Thatcher had already lost one of the Conservative Party's most popular ministers, Michael Heseltine, in 1986, as a result of her lack of sympathy with Europe. The resignation of Lawson was another serious blow. But it was the resignation of Howe which finally proved her undoing. This was precipitated by Thatcher's conduct at the Rome Council in October 1990, and, even more, by her hysterical remarks in reporting back to the Commons [*Doc. 15a*]. Howe's resignation speech was the more devastating because of the reputation for mildness and loyalty of its author. At the heart of his argument was the contention that Thatcher's scaremongering served only to increase the real danger to Britain's position – that of 'minimising our influence and maximising our chances of being once again shut out' [*Doc. 15b*]. The following day, Heseltine announced his decision to challenge Thatcher for the leadership. After failing to secure a clear victory on the first ballot, Thatcher reluctantly accepted the advice of her colleagues, and withdrew from the contest.

Europe was by no means the only reason why Thatcher lost the support of her party. The Thatcherite economic miracle was failing, the poll tax was a disaster, her authoritarian style of government alienated both colleagues and the general public, and opinion polls showed that she was unlikely to lead her party to a fourth successive victory. Nevertheless, Europe was more than just a trigger: for many of Thatcher's colleagues, it was the major reason why she had to go.

Sean Greenwood has suggested that Thatcher's European partners deliberately manoeuvred her into a position of isolation in order to undermine her [38 *p. 117*]. Whether this was the case or not, it was certainly true that the movement towards European integration was too strong for her to resist: at most, she 'succeeded in delaying rather than diverting the tide of events' [14 *pp. 255–6*].

9 THE MAJOR GOVERNMENTS, 1990–97

John Major was perhaps an unlikely candidate for the premiership. He was relatively inexperienced and by no means charismatic. This did not mean that he was unambitious, however. He was credited with an unusual feel for Conservative Party management, and had avoided committing himself to any of the factions into which the parliamentary party had increasingly fragmented. While many Thatcherites voted for him as the candidate most likely to beat Heseltine, his appeal was by no means confined to the supporters of the former prime minister. In terms of character, he was Thatcher's opposite: emollient, equable, and pragmatic. Throughout the first few years of his administration his personal popularity remained astonishingly high. This enabled him to turn around the enormous lead which Labour had built in the opinion polls, and in April 1992 – against the odds, and contrary to most expectations – to achieve a fourth successive Conservative election victory. His Commons majority was reduced to 21, however, and was further diminished by a series of by-election defeats. This added to the problems of party management bequeathed by the Thatcher years and by so long a period in power. By the time Major's second term came to an end, in 1997, the Conservative Party had itself become unelectable, and Major's own popularity had plummeted. European issues played a central part in these developments [173].

THE MAASTRICHT TREATY

Thatcher's downfall was greeted with barely concealed glee in Brussels and in the other capitals of Britain's European partners. Expectations of a change of approach were encouraged by a series of conciliatory moves: Michael Howard's more positive attitude to EC social legislation, Norman Lamont's altered tone on monetary union, Hurd's suggestion of increased co-operation in foreign policy, and finally Major's declaration that he wished to see Britain 'where we belong', 'at the very heart of Europe, working with our partners in building the future' [36 *p. 231*]. Nevertheless, on a number of important issues, such as the EC's policy in the 'Uruguay round' of GATT trade talks, or the conditions for enlargement of the EC, there were early indications that Britain continued to be out of step with the majority of its partners.

At Strasbourg in December 1989, and then at Dublin in June 1990, Thatcher had been unable to prevent her European partners setting in motion the machinery for two intergovernmental conferences (IGCs), on monetary and political union respectively. Thatcher argued that the IGCs were unnecessary, and that in the wake of the profound changes in eastern Europe, enlargement should be the EC's priority. The other governments argued that enlargement – and, more immediately, German reunification – should be accompanied by a strengthening and deepening of EC integration, to prevent the changes from fatally weakening EC cohesion. Fear that Thatcher's unconstructive attitude would sideline Britain in the negotiations was an important factor in precipitating her downfall. Nevertheless, Major's government followed a line which was little different from Thatcher's.

In the IGC on monetary union, Lamont continued to press for a solution first outlined by Major when Chancellor – that the ecu should develop into a 'hard' currency, parallel to the existing national currencies. The other governments were determined to create a single currency, to replace the existing currencies. In May 1991, perhaps out of exasperation, Delors suggested that Britain should be allowed to 'opt out' of the agreement on monetary union. This proposal was accepted by the British government, and embodied in the Maastricht Treaty* agreed by the European Council in December 1991. For the other EC states, the Treaty set strict 'convergence criteria' (relating to inflation rates, long-term interest rates, exchange-rate stability, and the size of budget deficits and public debt) which had to be satisfied before they could join the single currency. 1 January 1999 was set as the deadline for its launch. Britain's 'opt-out' was hailed as a triumph by government spokesmen, but failed to satisfy right-wing critics, who argued that Britain would have to help pay for the weaker EC countries to participate even if it stayed out, and also that Britain would find it difficult to stay out unless monetary union were pursued in a framework separate from the EC. The 'opt-out' also failed to satisfy many pro-Europeans, including leading figures in industry and finance.

The outcome of the IGC on political union was also unsatisfactory for Britain. Other countries were keen to extend majority voting to many aspects of social affairs, including welfare rights and employment law. The British government rejected such a move. Indeed, the government had already made clear its opposition to EC directives on such matters as working hours and maternity leave, which the Commission had introduced as health and safety matters subject to majority voting under the Single European Act. No solution to this problem had been found by the time of the Maastricht Council. Eventually, at Kohl's suggestion, Britain was offered what was effectively a second 'opt-out'. The Social Chapter* was dropped from the Treaty, and replaced by a protocol which allowed the eleven other EC members to use the EC machinery to pursue a common policy without Britain.

Some EC countries, notably France and Germany, were also keen to include foreign and security policy within the EC's remit. They argued that the EC's failure to develop a common and effective policy on the Gulf and Yugoslav conflicts pointed to the need for such integration. Britain, supported by other countries, notably Italy, argued that EC disagreements showed that a common foreign policy (especially one subject to majority voting) would be premature, and that a common security policy would undermine NATO. The latter point was also put, forcefully, by President Bush. The Maastricht Treaty referred to 'the eventual framing of a common defence policy [via the WEU], which might in time lead to a common defence', as well as providing for increased intergovernmental co-operation in foreign affairs. Nevertheless, the Treaty was 'arguably nearer to the British–Italian than to the Franco–German position' on this issue [36 *p. 253*].

The question of institutional reform was the most vexed of the questions which came before the IGC on political union. The draft Treaty produced by the Luxembourg presidency in April 1991 envisaged a 'European Union' (EU)* with three 'pillars': a reformed EC, inter-governmental co-operation on justice and home affairs, and intergovernmental co-operation on common foreign and security policy. The Dutch presidency produced a more federalist draft in September, which envisaged bringing the latter two areas within the normal EC machinery. In the subsequent bargaining, Britain was successful to the extent that the final Treaty resembled the Luxembourg more than the Dutch draft. This meant that justice and home affairs, and common foreign and security policy, were dealt with by separate intergovernmental machinery from which the European Commission, Court and Parliament were largely excluded. Britain was also successful in removing references to the 'federal' goal of the European Union. Finally, the Treaty referred for the first time to the necessity of 'respecting the principle of subsidiarity', which it defined as the principle of extending Community competence 'only if and in so far as the objectives of the proposed action cannot be sufficiently achieved by the Member States' [168 *p. 27*]. Nevertheless, the Maastricht Treaty also included a number of important steps in the direction of supranational integration. Majority voting in the Council of Ministers was extended further. The European Parliament was given significant new powers. Symbolically, the Treaty established a new citizenship of the European Union, which suggested 'the existence of a common popular sovereignty to complement – or rival – the common sovereignty of the states' [168 *p. 29*]. Finally, the Treaty committed the EU states to a further IGC in 1996, to examine the workings of the Treaty and suggest further institutional reform [18, 168].

John Major understandably chose to play down the supranational elements of the Maastricht Treaty. Indeed, he suggested that the three-pillar structure entrenched intergovernmentalism, and that Britain's 'opt-outs' on monetary union and social affairs made it 'game, set and match' for his government [170]. This satisfied neither his anti- nor his pro-European critics. The latter observed that the notion of a 'two-speed' Europe had now become a reality. John Major's subsequent attempt to make a virtue of this, by referring to the need for a Europe of 'variable geometry', did little to re-assure them.

BLACK WEDNESDAY

In her last speech in the House of Commons, in November 1991, Thatcher called for Britain to quit the ERM, which she now described as a trap leading inevitably to membership of a single currency. Within a year Britain had indeed left the ERM, although in circumstances far more humiliating than those envisaged by Thatcher. The reason was speculative pressure on the pound, fuelled by the unrealistically high level at which Britain had entered the mechanism, and by Britain's continuing economic problems, high German interest rates, a decline in the value of the dollar and uncertainty over Maastricht ratification. In 1991 Major instructed the head of his policy unit to draw up secret plans for a devaluation of sterling within the ERM. These were never implemented. Instead, when pressure mounted in the autumn of 1992, Major made a bombastic speech ruling out devaluation, while Lamont attempted to bully the President of the German *Bundesbank* into reducing German interest rates. The pressure came to a head on 'Black Wednesday', 16 September, when the government was at last forced to float the pound and thus effectively end British membership of the ERM. It is estimated that the government spent some £8 billion in the fruitless attempt to maintain the pound's value.

Britain's exit (and that of Italy, which occurred at the same time) severely weakened the ERM. The following year, massive spending by the *Bundesbank* averted the catastrophe of France leaving the system, but Spain and Portugal were also forced to leave the mechanism. Further speculation forced a widening of the ERM margins from 2.25 per cent to a virtually meaningless 15 per cent, in August 1993. Thereafter the ERM continued, but it increasingly resembled a Deutschmark zone. The conclusion drawn in the capitals of 'little Europe' was that only full monetary union could ensure sustained financial stability. France, in particular, pressed for this solution, as a means of regaining control over its monetary policy. The conclusion drawn in Britain was the opposite. 'Black Wednesday' led to an outburst of anti-German feeling, fuelled Conservative 'Euroscepticism' and diminished the already small possibility that Britain would seek to join monetary union. The effect of the crisis on Major's own credibility was considerable. This was compounded by his refusal to apologise or accept responsibility for the episode. Only two months later he did sack Lamont, but this only added to his woes, as Lamont immediately became one of his fiercest and most bitter critics [173].

A TREATY TOO FAR?

The Maastricht Treaty was agreed in December 1991 and signed in February 1992, but it was not ratified by Britain until 2 August 1993. The ratification debate was not only protracted. For the Conservative Party it was also deeply divisive. During the debate, Major frequently asserted that the Treaty involved relatively minor changes. This was not the interpretation put forward by Delors, however, who insisted that the Treaty was a major step towards a federal Europe. Nor was Major's interpretation shared by Thatcher, who declared Maastricht to be 'a treaty too far'. Thatcher's stance gave a lead to a growing number of Conservative 'Eurosceptics' – who were strengthened by the fact that European integration now became unprecedentedly unpopular even in the 'core' countries of 'little Europe'. The Germans feared losing the stability of the mark, and insisted on establishing a long-term 'stability pact' to reinforce the 'convergence criteria'. In France and elsewhere, the reforms necessary to meet the criteria created economic hardship and political dislocation.

Major presented the Maastricht agreement to Parliament in December 1991, but delayed the parliamentary debate until May 1992. This was a near-fatal mistake, because it gave critics of the Treaty time to organise and also put British ratification at the mercy of events elsewhere. The parliamentary debate was indeed suspended almost as soon as it began, after the Danes narrowly rejected the Treaty in a referendum held on 2 June. The Danish result gave encouragement to the 'Eurosceptics', who now accorded the demand for a British referendum a central place in their arguments [*Doc. 16a*]. Britain's EC presidency, which began in July 1991, was dominated by concern to find a solution to the Danish problem. Eventually this resulted in a solemn re-affirmation of the principle of subsidiarity, and a series of opt-outs for the Danes, agreed at the Edinburgh Council in December. Re-negotiation, which may have been Major's preferred option, was ruled out by the attitude of the other EC governments. Meanwhile, the ratification process had been further buffeted by the events of 'Black Wednesday', and by the narrowness of the margin by which the French accepted the Treaty in a referendum four days later.

On 4 November a government paving motion was carried, but with a bare majority of three. Twenty-six Conservatives voted against the government, and a further six abstained. It soon emerged that Major had only obtained this majority by promising that final ratification would not take place until after the second Danish referendum. The Labour Party, meanwhile, was solid. Not only was this seen as a possible opportunity to oust the government, but the only part of the Treaty for which Labour felt much enthusiasm – the social protocol – was the subject of one of Major's 'opt-outs'. Worse was to come. The committee stage of the bill involved some 210 hours' debate spread over 23 days, and the consideration of more than 600 amendments. The government was forced to use every weapon at its disposal in order to limit its major defeats to one. On 17 May the second Danish referendum at last approved the Treaty, allowing the government to move the third reading of the bill. On 25 May, forty-one Conservatives voted against, and a further five abstained. The majority of Labour MPs abstained, however, since the government had been forced to accept a separate vote on the social protocol 'opt-out'. This duly took place on 22 July, resulting in a vote of 324 to 316 against the government's policy. The following day, Major faced a vote of confidence, declaring that it was now necessary to 'lance the boil' of Conservative divisions on Europe. The prospect of facing a general election at a time when Labour was twenty points ahead in the opinion polls, and in which they themselves might be deprived of party endorsement, ensured that, with one exception, the Conservative 'Eurosceptics' now ended their rebellion [166].

THE CONSERVATIVE PARTY DIVIDED

The ratification of the Maastricht Treaty marked the end only of one stage in Major's difficulties over Europe. It certainly did not mark the end of Conservative 'Euroscepticism'. Hostility to the EU (as it now became) characterised the attitudes not only of longstanding back-bench anti-Europeans, such as Bill Cash and Teddy Taylor, but of the former prime minister and numerous of her colleagues, and also of younger Cabinet ministers, notably Michael Portillo and John Redwood. Their relative importance was magnified not only by the smallness of the government's parliamentary majority, but also by the solid support which they were given by the jingoistic and frequently xenophobic popular press. Economic arguments played only a small part in their hostility to the EU, although it was frequently asserted that Europe was irreversibly wedded to over-regulation and centralised direction. The key arguments for the 'Eurosceptics' concerned security, prosperity and sovereignty – issues which had lain 'at the heart of the Conservatives' successful appeal to the mass electorate' since 1979 [166 *pp.* 46–7]. According to the 'Eurosceptics', the EU had been taken over by continental federalists (most notably Delors), who were now using every opportunity to force Britain into unwanted further integration. It was necessary not only to say 'no' to further integration, but also to 'repatriate' powers which had already been transferred.

The extent of Conservative divisions on Europe was brought home to the general public by the disclosure of Major's off-the-cuff remarks to a journalist at the time of the July 1993 confidence debate, in which he referred to his 'Eurosceptic' colleagues as 'bastards'. In November 1994 a rebellion on the question of EU resources resulted in the Conservative whip being withdrawn from a number of prominent anti-Europeans. The effect on the government (which technically lost its majority) appears to have been more serious than on the 'Eurosceptics' themselves, who succeeded in extracting significant concessions before returning to the fold. In June 1995 Major again tried to 'lance the boil' by announcing that he would submit himself to a leadership contest. Redwood promptly obliged by throwing his hat in the ring. Although Major won, the predominant impression given by the contest was one of prime ministerial weakness and a Conservative Party riven to the core.

Major's outburst against the 'Eurosceptics' was only one side of the story. The other was a steady and continuous drift towards their position. In March 1994 he picked a quarrel with his EU partners on the question of changes to 'qualified' majority voting following enlargement – but then was forced to back down. He then authorised a highly negative campaign during the European elections in June the same year – but again was humiliated, by the Conservatives' worst-ever European election performance [*Doc. 19*]. Undeterred, Major picked another quarrel with all eleven of his partners the following month, vetoing the appointment of the Belgian Jean-Luc Dehaene as Delors' successor, and insisting instead on the Luxembourg Prime Minister Jacques Santer. Once again Major shot himself in the foot: Santer was more of a federalist than Dehaene, and was annoyed by Major's characterisation of him as the weaker of the two. At the Dublin Council in December 1996, Major blocked progress on a number of important issues but was overruled on others. Britain was 'the grit in the EU oyster', he rather inappropriately declared.

Major's response to the rise of 'Euroscepticism' dismayed a number of more mainstream Conservative figures, including Heseltine, Hurd and Kenneth Clarke (Lamont's successor as Chancellor). Clarke memorably described the 'Eurosceptics' as acting like 'a barrel-load of monkeys'. That Conservative divisions on Europe were also beginning to frighten business was made clear by a letter to *The Financial Times* on the eve of the 1997 election, in which a number of Britain's most prominent business leaders attacked 'the mistaken belief that an arm's length and hostile attitude on Europe is now in the UK's best interests' [*Doc. 16b*]. As the election approached, the divisions within the Conservative Party appeared to widen. Partly this was a response to the threat posed by the Referendum Party, which ran candidates against non-'Eurosceptic' Conservatives. Founded and led by Sir James Goldsmith, a multi-millionaire MEP (representing a coalition of French right-wing extremists), the Referendum Party was estimated to have a 'war-chest' of £20 million, and caused considerable anxiety amongst previously uncommitted Conservatives. During the election campaign, Major was unable to prevent numerous MPs from issuing their own 'Eurosceptic' manifestoes, sometimes in contradiction to the official Conservative manifesto. The overall impression was of a party tearing itself apart.

10 THE BLAIR GOVERNMENT, 1997–

Major clung to power until very nearly the last possible date for a general election, in the hope that something might turn up to retrieve his position. On the contrary, the delay merely allowed Conservative divisions to fester, and a series of corruption scandals to emerge. The result was devastating: the lowest Conservative share of the vote this century (reducing the parliamentary party by more than half), and a landslide Labour majority of 179. Some Conservatives drew comfort from the fact that the Referendum Party proved a busted flush, gaining no more than 3 per cent of the vote. Nevertheless, an extra nineteen Conservative MPs would have retained their seats had the votes cast for anti-European parties gone to them, and in a more closely-fought election the number might have been higher. Major immediately resigned as Conservative leader, and William Hague emerged to succeed him, defeating both Redwood and Clarke. Like Major, Hague was a compromise candidate, not identified with any particular wing of the party. Nevertheless, he signalled the Conservatives' continued drift towards anti-Europeanism by an early decision to rule out support for membership of a single currency for at least ten years. This was immediately attacked by Clarke and Heseltine but was largely ignored by the media and general public. For the moment, the Conservatives no longer appeared to matter.

NEW LABOUR, NEW EUROPE?

The 1997 election was a triumph for the 'modernisation' of the Labour Party begun by Neil Kinnock and carried through by John Smith and Tony Blair, and it illustrated the extent to which the party had learned the lessons of its 1983 defeat [171]. The process was symbolised by the surreptitious yet decisive way in which the party began to present itself as 'New Labour'. In organisational terms this meant unprecedented party unity and the concentration of power in the hands of the leader; in presentational terms it meant slick publicity and the ascendance of 'spin doctors'; in policy terms it meant the abandonment of old-fashioned socialism and the adoption of Thatcherite measures in education, social security and other areas, from which even Thatcher herself had shrunk. 'New Labour' attitudes to Europe were also the opposite of those of 1983 [169]. In 1992, the Labour Party fought the election on a manifesto which promised to 'promote Britain out of the European second division into which our country has been relegated by the Tories' [*Doc. 17c*]. In 1997 Labour's commitment to Europe was made yet clearer still. The Conservatives, the manifesto claimed, had left Britain 'on the sidelines'. Labour, by contrast, would assume 'a leading role' [*Doc. 17d*].

As on numerous occasions in recent British history, the question which naturally arose was, to what extent the change in the government's tone on Europe indicated a real change in substance. Here, the early indications were by no means entirely positive. Indeed, even the change of tone on Europe appears, by a curious paradox, to have been designed more for domestic consumption than with the aim of convincing Britain's European partners. Blair caused considerable resentment at a meeting of European socialists soon after the election, by presuming to lecture them on their supposed failings – which consisted almost entirely of their attachment to old-fashioned socialism. The election of a socialist government in France did nothing to make relations easier. More generally, Blair's confident talk of 'leading Europe' was widely resented, coming from a country which, after nearly 25 years of membership, had yet to establish its European credentials. This was especially the case in relation to monetary union, the biggest single project of the EU, and one which looked likely to dominate the EU agenda into the next century. That a Labour government would not carry through a major change in British policy in this area had been indicated as early as January 1996, when Blair declared that 'the British people are not yet ready to accept a single European currency'. In November 1996 he promised that Labour would hold a referendum before joining a single currency; and in September 1997 Gordon Brown, the new Chancellor, made clear that a Labour government would not be recommending joining within the lifetime of the 1997 parliament – in other words, before 2002. Labour's negative stance did not prevent Blair from demanding a seat on the committee which would shape future monetary policy, at the Luxembourg Council in December 1997. France in particular opposed such a concession: Britain would then have power without responsibility, a desirable but not a wholly justifiable position.

THE AMSTERDAM TREATY

The intergovernmental conference (IGC) envisaged by the Maastricht Treaty was launched at Turin in March 1996. The then Conservative government produced a White Paper which was almost wholly negative in tone: not only did it oppose any strengthening of EU institutions, it also proposed repatriating some powers and reversing earlier decisions on majority voting. Virtually the only positive note was that 'there may be some areas where it is perfectly healthy for some member states to integrate more closely or more quickly than others' [172 *p. 6*]. British obstruction ensured that progress in the IGC was slow. Many of Britain's partners openly expressed the hope that an election would remove Major's government from power. Meanwhile, the Italian, Irish and Dutch presidencies attempted to proceed on a basis of 'fifteen minus one'.

Blair kept in close touch with developments in the IGC, especially through contacts with the Dutch premier, Wim Kok. These enabled his government to 'hit the ground running' after 1 May. The British election broke the logjam in the IGC and the draft of a new Treaty was agreed at the Amsterdam Council on 19 June. Under this Treaty, Britain agreed to the incorporation of the social protocol into the normal EU machinery, although a veto was still retained on matters relating to employment law. The machinery for a common foreign and security policy was also strengthened, although again the veto was retained. Majority voting was extended to a range of new issues, however, and the European Parliament was given a greater legislative role. In addition, the EU was given a new role in relation to 'fundamental rights', and EU member-states promised to co-operate in 'developing a co-ordinated strategy for employment and particularly for promoting a skilled, trained and adaptable workforce' [*The Times*, 18 Nov. 1996, *p. 6*]. A proposal by the French government to provide significant new funds for employment creation was blocked, however, partly by Blair himself.

In presenting the results of the Amsterdam Council to Parliament, Blair emphasised that 'for the first time in a decade Britain is setting a positive agenda for Europe'. Nevertheless, he also emphasised that his government had 'ensured continued protection for our essential interests in all the areas in which we sought it' [*Doc. 18*]. While Blair had ended one 'opt-out', on the social protocol, he now negotiated another – on the incorporation of the Schengen agreement (covering border controls, immigration and asylum policy) into the normal EU machinery. He presented this as an 'opt-in', in that Britain could choose to go along with decisions made by the other member-states, but the distinction was subtle. Another area in which he ensured continued protection for British interests was in relation to the principle of 'variable geometry' – or 'flexibility', as it was now termed. Unlike Major, he regarded this as a threat to British interests, and succeeded in retaining a veto over the use of EU machinery by inner groups of states [167].

The IGC had originally been summoned to resolve the institutional question, in preparation for the enlargement of the EU from fifteen to twenty or twenty-five states. Nevertheless, little was achieved in this field. The whole question of weighted votes and blocking minorities in the Council of Ministers was shelved, while the issue of a 'democratic deficit' arising from the arcane intergovernmental machinery at the heart of the EU was largely ignored – much to the disappointment of the European Parliament. It was agreed, however, that a new IGC would be called at least a year before the next round of enlargement. This ensured that the institutional question (and the related questions of federalism and the diminution of national sovereignty) looked likely to remain firmly on the EU agenda into the next century.

11 THE LONG ROAD TO EUROPE

Alan Milward has argued that the process of European integration was undertaken, paradoxically, in an attempt to 'rescue the nation-state'. In an age of increasing economic and political interdependence, and therefore of nation-state vulnerability, national governments 'pooled' their sovereignty in order to protect national interests and extend their control of their own destinies. In all the 'core' European countries which formed the ECSC and later the EEC, national interests dictated such a move. In Germany and Italy, the motive was primarily to safeguard democracy; in France, it was to control Germany; in Belgium, the Netherlands and Luxembourg, it was to gain influence over policies which would affect them greatly. In Britain, by contrast, national interests dictated a different line, and it was only when exclusion from the Communities appeared to threaten national interests that British governments began to accept the need for membership. The very different motivation behind British entry ensured that the aims of British governments once inside the Communities would be limited and 'defensive' [20].

This interpretation has been supported by those studies of British policy which have so far appeared. Sean Greenwood has emphasised that British governments before the 1960s were following British interests in staying out of the emergent Communities [38]. John Young has illustrated the extent to which Bevin and Eden did have positive policies towards Europe, but ones which sought the development of European cooperation by means of 'practical programmes' rather than 'ambitious schemes' [45]. Finally, Stephen George has argued that successive British governments, both before and after 1973, and both Conservative and Labour, have pursued a consistent policy of attempting to pursue regional co-operation on strictly intergovernmental lines, and attempting to prevent 'regionalism' from disrupting 'globalism' and 'internationalism' [37, 170].

The effects of this difference in approach between Britain and the 'core' countries of Europe have been profound. In Britain, there has been little enthusiasm for European integration *per se*, and equally little understanding of the enthusiasm felt on the continent. European integration has been seen as a menace rather than an opportunity, and very few British politicians have attempted to argue (as is commonplace on the continent) that monetary union, for instance, is the only way of regaining control over financial policy. The European idea of pursuing economic integration as a means to political union has also been met with blank incomprehension, if not outright hostility. Britain has always been attempting to slow down the process of integration and, consequently, has often fallen behind and had no choice but to catch up.

BRITAIN'S ROLE IN EUROPE

During the momentous Commons debate on British entry into the European Community, on 28 October 1971, Heath declared that in future relations between Britain and Europe would no longer be a question of 'them' and 'us': 'We are approaching the point where, if this House so decides tonight, it will become just as much our Community as their Community' [35 *p. 240*]. The tendency to think in terms of 'them' and 'us' proved considerably more resilient than Heath anticipated – and considerably more useful to British politicians. At times the popular press appeared to sense the existence of a rich minefield of popular xenophobia, to be tapped in the battle for circulation. This was frequently fed by stories of some latest European threat – a proposal to outlaw flavoured crisps, undersized tomatoes, or the British oak. Such stories usually proved to be the product of overheated imagination, or else the result of a peculiar or over-zealous interpretation of EU law by some British civil servant. In 1996 the European Commission was reported to be considering setting up a special unit to refute such stories. Their very existence indicated the prevalence of attitudes of suspicion and mistrust, but also a misunderstanding of the nature of the EU machinery – which, at the very least, required the approval of a majority of national governments, and in all important cases required the approval of all national governments, before common measures could be imposed.

Whether popular attitudes were quite as hostile to European integration as the press and certain politicians appeared to assume is open to question. The effects of the rise of 'Euroscepticism' within the Conservative Party suggested that they were not. The only attempt to gauge popular attitudes properly was the 1975 referendum. This, of course, produced an overwhelming vote in favour of continued membership. Opponents of membership claimed that in 1975 the public had been deceived. This is difficult to square with the vigorous debate which surrounded the referendum, in which opponents of membership had their fair say. Later, it was claimed – by Thatcher, among others – that changes in the EC/EU had invalidated the referendum result. In Thatcher's view, the EC was originally an intergovernmental arrangement which had subsequently been hijacked as part of a federalist plot. There are substantial reasons for rejecting such a view. Federalist ideas, unlike the British government, had been 'present at the creation'. Economic integration was pursued explicitly for political reasons. The goal of an 'ever closer union' was embodied in the Treaties of Rome.

The present EU is, as lawyers would say, *sui generis*. It is not yet a federation. Nor is it, or has it ever been, a piece of purely intergovernmental machinery. But it is likely that it will continue to evolve in a federalist direction. As understood on the continent, federalism involves taking decisions at the most appropriate level. Many of Britain's partners believe that a federal system would be more logical, efficient, transparent, accountable and democratic than the present system, which involves leaving enormous power in the hands of politicians elected on issues entirely unrelated to the questions dealt with at a European level. It is likely that the project of monetary union and the attempt to create a common foreign policy will raise the question of accountability in an acute form and lead to pressure to move further in the federalist direction.

The British government's response to this cannot be predicted. A consistent pattern has emerged since 1945, however, of British governments initially standing aloof from the latest thrust of integration, then finding themselves on the sidelines, then being forced to join in when the mould has been set and it has been difficult to shape the emergent institutions and policies in a form more compatible with British interests. British national interests have clearly been damaged by this behaviour. Britain's influence in Europe has inevitably been less than it might have been. This has had an important knock-on effect on Britain's influence elsewhere. Before the 1960s successive British governments cited the Anglo-American relationship as one reason why Britain could not join Europe, yet Britain's refusal to do so was a source of irritation and at times a strain in the relationship. After British entry, even Thatcher's 'special' relationship with President Reagan could not prevent a continuing shift in American policy towards seeing Germany and France as the key European actors and therefore the most important of America's European partners.

THE EFFECTS OF BRITISH MEMBERSHIP

It would be well-nigh impossible to draw up a balance sheet of the economic costs and benefits to Britain of EC/EU membership. Britain's net contribution to the European budget – that is, the difference between British contributions to the EU in the form of direct subventions and 'own resources', and British receipts in the form of spending from the agricultural, regional and other funds – has, of course, been quantified, and is used as the basis for calculating British refunds [*Doc. 12b*]. Against this must be set the amount that Britain has gained from access to the European common market. This, by its very nature, is unquantifiable. Moreover, any realistic assessment of costs and benefits would have to consider the alternative, but it is by no means clear how the British economy would have fared outside the common market, or indeed how the EC/EU itself might have developed had Britain not become a member.

What is clear, is that since 1945 there has been a decisive shift in British trade patterns, away from the Commonwealth and towards western Europe. In 1948, the countries which constituted the Communities in 1973 ('the Six', Ireland and Denmark) accounted for 13.1 per cent of Britain's imports and took 16.7 per cent of British exports. In 1983 the comparable figures were 45.6 per cent and 43.8 per cent [16 *p. 150*]. By 1987, the EC accounted for more than half of British trade. By 1997 the figure was nearer 60 per cent. Catherine Schenck has emphasised that the shift was merely accelerated, not caused, by Britain's EC membership [141]. The crucial point is perhaps that Britain is now economically dependent on its trade with western Europe. British membership of the EC/EU has brought considerable opportunities for the expansion of trade; conversely, British withdrawal (and the imposition of EC tariffs on British goods) would cause significant damage to British trade and hence to the British economy as a whole. At the time of Britain's first application to join the Communities, it was argued by some that the Commonwealth or even the North Atlantic offered possibilities of a free trade area from which Britain could benefit. As the Wilson government found, such ideas proved illusions. At the same time, Britain's experience in the GATT trade talks illustrated the precariousness of a position outside any trading bloc.

One of the factors which impelled Britain to seek EC membership in the 1960s was the disparity between British economic growth rates and those of 'the Six'. Britain was unfortunate in entering the EC just when the economic crisis of the 1970s began to take effect. EC membership was therefore associated with economic dislocation and recession rather than growth. In the 1980s, Britain achieved an average growth rate of 2.2 per cent a year, compared with 2.1 per cent for France [30 *p. 237*]. This was a function of many factors, of which EC trade creation was only one. Nevertheless, EC membership also played a crucial role in attracting investment from abroad. In 1991, 53 per cent of all Japanese direct investment in the EC came to Britain. This was attracted by the deregulatory policies (leading to low wages and labour 'flexibility') pursued by the then Conservative government, but had Britain 'not been a member, then there is little doubt that the investment would have gone elsewhere, to a site inside the EC' [37 *p. 95*].

Arguably, it has been in the political rather than the economic sphere that the effects of British membership have been most significant, as well as most controversial. The areas in which the EC/EU has been authorised to act have expanded enormously since 1958. Britain, like other EC/EU member-states, has been committed by the Treaties of Rome to giving precedence to EC/EU law in such areas. This has meant a substantial erosion of the traditional British legal and parliamentary system. An illustration of this occurred in 1990 when the European Court of Justice ordered British courts to suspend the Merchant Shipping Act of 1988, while it heard a case brought by Spanish fishermen. There was no precedent for this in British law, and no machinery for suspending parliamentary legislation other than by a further Act of Parliament. The machinery had to be invented, with the House of Lords as the highest court of the land duly suspending a law which it had itself previously approved [36 *p. 222*]. Critics of the EC/EU frequently argue that the European Court and Commission are constantly on the look-out for ways in which to increase their power [31]. Be that as it may, the impact of EC/EU law has been enormous. There are now few British government departments which are not bound by EU decisions and therefore involved in continuous negotiation at a European level. This in turn has had an effect on the policy-making process more generally. Many British lobbies and pressure groups now maintain a significant presence in Brussels [15 *p. 377*].

The most controversial aspect of Britain's membership of the EU relates to this 'erosion' of national sovereignty. Britain is now constrained by the EU machinery to the extent that many of the most important decisions affecting the British people are made in Brussels rather than London. But, as David Reynolds has pointed out in relation to Thatcher's outbursts on the subject, an assertion of national sovereignty is to a certain extent 'unreal'. If one is to talk of 'losing' national sovereignty, then national sovereignty is lost every time a country concludes a diplomatic agreement. In these terms, British membership of NATO has been the most significant 'loss' of national sovereignty this century [14 *p. 273*]. Geoffrey Howe put the same point in a speech delivered before his resignation in 1990. Sovereignty, he argued, was 'not some pre-defined absolute', but 'a resource to be used'. The 'pooling' of sovereignty increased a nation's capacity to exercise influence in the world. The EC he thus compared to a rope made of twelve skeins, each retaining its individual quality but gaining in strength by its engagement with the others [39]. The question which naturally arises when the 'loss' of sovereignty is discussed is, 'What is the alternative?'. In an age of interdependence, an insistence on national sovereignty may actually diminish a nation's capacity to attain its objectives. Conversely, the 'pooling' of sovereignty is in many areas the most effective, and in some areas the only, way of exercising it [44].

PART FOUR: DOCUMENTS

ANGLO-FRENCH UNION: THE 'CHURCHILL PROPOSAL' (16 JUNE 1940)

The extremities of war led Churchill's Cabinet to approve a proposal for a far-reaching 'Franco-British Union'. This proposal was transmitted to the French government at 4.30pm on Sunday 16 June 1940. The French Prime Minister, Paul Reynaud, was in favour of acceptance but his colleagues demurred. Reynaud resigned and at half-past midnight Marshal Pétain initiated the negotiations leading to the French surrender.

At this most fateful moment in the history of the modern world the Governments of the United Kingdom and the French Republic make this declaration of indissoluble union and unyielding resolution in their common defence of justice and freedom against subjection to a system which reduces mankind to a life of robots and slaves.

The two Governments declare that France and Great Britain shall no longer be two nations, but one Franco-British Union.

The constitution of the Union will provide for joint organs of defence, foreign, financial, and economic policies.

Every citizen of France will enjoy immediately citizenship of Great Britain; every British subject will become a citizen of France.

Both countries will share responsibility for the repair of the devastation of war, wherever it occurs in their territories, and the resources of both shall be equally, and as one, applied to that purpose ...

The Union will concentrate its whole energy against the power of the enemy, no matter where the battle may be.

And thus we shall conquer.

Winston Churchill, *The Second World War*, Vol. 2, *Their Finest Hour*, Cassell, London, 1949, pp. 183–4.

DOCUMENT 2   BEVIN AND EUROPE

Ernest Bevin has sometimes been portrayed as 'anti-European'. However, as these extracts show, Bevin was in favour of a considerable degree of western European integration. In document (a), Bevin outlines his 'grand design' at a meeting of senior Foreign Office officials on 13 August 1945. Document (b) is from his speech to the House of Commons on 22 January 1948, in which he describes his strategy for 'Western Union'.

(a) The Secretary of State explained that his long-term policy was to establish close relations between this country and the countries on the Mediterranean and Atlantic fringes of Europe – e.g. more especially Greece, Italy, France, Belgium, the Netherlands and Scandinavia. He wanted to see close association between the United Kingdom and these countries – as much in commercial and economic matters as in political questions. It was necessary to make a start with France, and he was therefore very anxious to put relations between this country and France onto a better footing as soon as possible. As a first step in this direction it seemed essential to endeavour to reach some agreement with the French Government over the question of the Levant States. ... As regards the further steps to be taken to improve relations with France, the Secretary of State explained that while he was anxious, as he had already said, to work towards a closer association between this country and the countries on the fringe of Europe, more particularly France, he did not wish to take any active steps towards the conclusion of a Franco-British alliance or the formation of a Western group until he had had more time to consider possible Russian reactions. He was anxious, however, that in the meantime everything possible should be done to improve our commercial and economic relations with France – and also if practicable with the other liberated countries in Western Europe. Unfortunately, just at the present time it was very difficult for the United Kingdom to help France and the other countries in this direction to any substantial extent.

Margaret Pelly, Heather Yasamee and Gillian Bennett (eds) [9], pp. 15–19.

(b) Surely all these developments which I have been describing, point to the conclusion that the free nations of Western Europe must now draw closely together. ... I hope that treaties will thus be signed with our near neighbours, the Benelux countries, making our treaty with France an important nucleus in Western Europe. We have then to go beyond the circle of our immediate neighbours. We shall have to consider the question of associating other historic members of European civilisation, including the new Italy, in this great conception. ... We are thinking now of Western Europe as a unit. ... We should do all we can to foster both the spirit and the machinery of cooperation. ... Britain cannot stand outside of Europe and regard her problems as quite separate from those of her European neighbours. ... I would emphasise that I am not concerned only with Europe as a geographical conception. Europe has extended its influence throughout the world, and we have to look further afield. ... The organisation of Western Europe must be economically supported. That involves the closest possible collaboration with the Commonwealth and with overseas territories, not only British but French, Dutch, Belgian and Portuguese. These overseas territories are large primary producers, and their standard of life is evolving rapidly and is capable of great development. They have raw materials, food and resources which can be turned to very great common advantage, both to the people of the territories themselves, to Europe, and to the world as a whole.

Parliamentary Debates (Hansard), House of Commons, 5th Series, Vol. 446, 22 January 1948, cols. 395–8.

DOCUMENT 3 CHURCHILL AND EUROPE

In contrast to Bevin, Churchill is often thought of as one of the 'founding fathers' of European integration. His speech at Zürich University on 19 September 1946 (a) gave an enormous impetus to the movement for a 'United States of Europe'. His qualification, that Britain and the Commonwealth could only be 'friends and sponsors' of the new Europe, was often ignored. Churchill clarified his views in a memorandum to the Cabinet, soon after taking office as leader of the new Conservative government in 1951 (b).

(a) I wish to speak to you today about the tragedy of Europe. This noble continent, comprising on the whole the fairest and the most cultivated regions of the earth, enjoying a temperate and equable climate, is the home of all the great parent races of the western world. It is the fountain of Christian faith and Christian ethics. It is the origin of most of the culture, arts, philosophy, and science both of ancient and modern times. If Europe were once united in the sharing of its common inheritance, there would be no limit to the happiness, to the prosperity and glory which its three or four hundred million people would enjoy. Yet it is from Europe that have sprung that series of frightful nationalistic quarrels, originated by the Teutonic nations, which we have seen even in this twentieth century and in our lifetime, wreck the peace and mar the prospects of all mankind. ...

I am now going to say something that will astonish you. The first step in the recreation of the European family must be a partnership between France and Germany. In this way only can France recover the moral leadership of Europe. There can be no revival of Europe without a spiritually great France and a spiritually great Germany. The structure of the United States of Europe, if well and truly built, will be such as to make the material strength of a single state less important. Small nations will count as much as large ones and gain their honour by their contribution to the common cause. ...

The first step is to form a Council of Europe. If at first all the states of Europe are not willing or able to join the union, we must nevertheless proceed to assemble and combine those who will and those who can. ... In all this urgent work, France and Germany must take the lead together. Great Britain, the British Commonwealth of Nations, mighty America, and I trust Soviet Russia – for then indeed all would be well – must be the friends and sponsors of the new Europe and must champion its right to live and shine.

Winston S. Churchill: His Complete Speeches, 1897–1963, Vol. VII, *1943–49*, ed. Robert Rhodes James, Chelsea House Publishers, 1974.

(b) It may simplify discussion if I set forth briefly my own view and the line I have followed so far.

1. At Zürich in 1946 I appealed to France to take the lead in Europe by making friends with the Germans, 'burying the thousand-year quarrel', &c. This caused a shock at the time but progress has been continual. I always recognised that, as Germany is potentially so much stronger than France, militarily and economically, Britain and if possible the United States should be associated with United Europe, to make an even balance and to promote the United Europe Movement.

2. ... I am not opposed to a European Federation including (eventually) the countries behind the Iron Curtain, provided that this comes about naturally and gradually. But I never thought that Britain or the British Commonwealth should, whether individually or collectively, become an integral part of a European Federation, and have never given the slightest support to the idea. ...

6. On the economic side, I welcome the Schuman Coal and Steel Plan as a step in the reconciliation of France and Germany, and as probably rendering another Franco-German war physically impossible. I never contemplated Britain joining in this plan on the same terms as Continental partners. We should, however, have joined in all the discussions, and had we done so not only a better plan would probably have emerged, but our own interests would have been watched at every stage. ...

7. Our first object is the unity and consolidation of the British Commonwealth and what is left of the former British Empire. Our second, the 'fraternal association' of the English-speaking world; and third, United Europe, to which we are a separate closely – and specially – related ally and friend.

Winston Churchill, Cabinet memorandum on 'United Europe', 29 November 1951 (PRO FCAB 129/48, c(51)32), in Lawrence Butler and Harriet Jones (eds) [5], pp. 226–8.

DOCUMENT 4   THE SCHUMAN PLAN AND THE ECSC

On 9 May 1950, the French Foreign Minister, Robert Schuman, announced a plan for a supranational authority to control Franco-German coal and steel production. He invited other governments to join the negotiations, but only on condition that they accept the supranational principle. In document (a), Sir Ivone Kirkpatrick, head of the German section of the Foreign Office, weighs up the advantages and disadvantages of joining the negotiations. The British Cabinet decided against doing so on 2 June, a decision criticised by, among others, The Economist (b).

(a) The French plan speaks only of France and Germany. But in his covering note the French Ambassador emphasises that it is designed to be a European plan. Yet he does not make it clear whether or not the participation of the United Kingdom is regarded as essential. If it is not to be essential and if economic factors do not *compel* us to come in or if we could devise some form of consultative association without full participation, the prospective close association of France and Germany would be politically attractive. ... But if the United Kingdom is required to join or if economic factors prevent our staying out, British participation is likely to involve us in Europe beyond the point of no return, whether the plan involves some form of immediate Federation in Europe or whether it is 'the first step in the Federation of Europe' as the French statement puts it or whether it is merely a species of European cartel. ... In any event it would be damaging to take the lead at the very outset in subjecting the plan to public criticism. It has had a good reception in many quarters including governmental circles in Germany and we cannot afford to be accused of wishing to torpedo a promising move towards Franco-German rapprochement.

Memorandum by Sir Ivone Kirkpatrick, 11 May 1950, in Roger Bullen and Margaret Pelly (eds) [1], pp. 34–5.

(b) One can regret that the issue was brought up by such unworthy tactics. One can regret that so mighty a principle as the pooling of sovereignty was invoked, and such high hopes of permanent pacification aroused, in support of a proposal which only those versed in its formidable technicalities can really understand – and whose actual practical accomplishments may yet turn out to be small. One can be deeply distrustful of the French and American leaning to the dangerous and difficult principle of federalism, and disappointed at the failure to realise how much sovereignty has already been pooled in defence matters by much less spectacular and more workmanlike methods, in which the British have been the reverse of backward.

But when all these things have been said, the fact remains that at the bar of world opinion, the Schuman proposal has become a test. And the British Government have failed it.

The Economist, 10 July 1950.

DOCUMENT 5   THE PLEVEN PLAN AND THE EDC

The Korean war brought to the fore the question of German rearmament, which Britain and America supported, but the French opposed. On 24 October 1950 the French Prime Minister, René Pleven, announced a plan for German rearmament in the context of a European army. Bevin was deeply hostile, suspecting a French attempt to undermine the Atlantic alliance (a). Nevertheless, he and his successor Herbert Morrison maintained a public attitude of benevolent neutrality. Anthony Eden, Conservative Foreign Secretary from October 1951, proposed to continue this attitude, while preparing for the plan's failure (b). The plan was indeed rejected by the French National Assembly, on 30 August 1954.

(a) One of the ideas underlying the French plan is, undoubtedly, that of a Continental bloc, under French leadership, which while linked with the Atlantic Community, would constitute in world politics a force with some measure of independence. Such a continental bloc ... might not only present certain dangers to ourselves if it were to adopt a policy of neutrality; it would also be in conflict with the basic principle of the Atlantic Treaty as a free association of 12 equal independent states. Such a bloc would be too feeble to defend itself and yet strong enough to assert itself in world politics. It would thus be a sort of cancer in the Atlantic body which would, I am afraid, constitute a serious disruptive element and might in the end endanger the Treaty itself: all the more so since it would be calculated to discourage instead of encouraging continuing American concern with the security of Europe.

Present French policy is, I believe, at bottom antipathetic towards NATO and to the Americans. The proposal for a European Army is only one of many aspects of this covert antipathy. There have recently been other signs of it in the economic field. If we are ever to break down this antipathy and to make the French good members of NATO, we cannot afford to allow the European federal concept to gain a foothold within NATO and thus weaken instead of strengthening the ties between the countries of the two sides of the Atlantic. We must nip it in the bud.

Memorandum by Ernest Bevin, 24 November 1950, in Roger Bullen and Margaret Pelly (eds) [3], pp. 291–6.

(b) Here are some comments:
1. At present there is only one plan under discussion for a European army.
2. This is the so-called Pleven Plan. This has made technical progress, but it is in political trouble over fundamental questions of sovereignty. This plan does not permit national armies to exist in participating countries, except for overseas garrisons. Its purpose, at least in French and Italian

minds, is to pave the way for federation. I have never thought it possible that we could join such an army.

3. The late Government made clear its attitude to the army, and to the Schuman Plan, in a joint statement by the Foreign Secretaries of France, the United States and the United Kingdom, at Washington in September. I quoted this in the House in my speech in the foreign affairs debate, and it was generally approved. ...

4. Now that the Pleven Plan is running into trouble in the countries that put it forward, we are being made the whipping boy.

Conclusion:

a) We should support the Pleven Plan, though we cannot be members of it. This is what the Americans are doing, and it is the course Eisenhower wants us to take.

b) If the Pleven Plan does collapse, we should try to work out a more modest scheme with our allies. ...

c) Any move for b) will require careful timing. If we move too soon, the Pleven Plan will collapse, and we shall be told we have killed it.

Letter from Eden to Churchill, 1 December 1951, in Anthony Eden, *Full Circle*, Cassell, London, 1960, pp. 33–4.

DOCUMENT 6   THE MESSINA CONFERENCE AND THE EEC

Within a year of the failure of the EDC proposal, the governments of 'the Six' agreed a 'rélance' of European integration, at the Messina conference of 1–3 June 1955. Britain was again invited to participate in the negotiations. In Cabinet, the Chancellor, R.A. (Rab) Butler, argued against full participation, with considerable support from his colleagues (a). Britain's efforts to negotiate a free trade area more in keeping with Britain's interests failed, however, leading even the relatively pro-European Harold Macmillan to consider an aggressive and belligerent response (b).

(a) The Chancellor of the Exchequer said that at Messina the six ECSC countries had resolved to make further advances towards the economic unification of Europe, and to invite the United Kingdom Government to take part in the work of a Preparatory Committee. Some of the specific objectives of the six Powers ... for example, the creation of a common organisation for the peaceful development of atomic energy and the establishment of a common market in Europe, seemed likely to involve duplication with other arrangements or were fraught with special difficulties. He therefore recommended that we should agree to take part in the work of the Preparatory Committee as observers only and subject to suitable reservations about our attitude to the specified objectives.

In discussion support was expressed for the view that the utmost caution was required on our part in relation to the specified objectives of the six ECSC countries. It was suggested, on the other hand, that we ought not to create the impression that we disapproved of their efforts to promote a greater measure of economic integration between themselves.

Minutes of Cabinet Meeting held on 30 June 1955 (PRO CAB 128/29, cm(55)19), in Sean Greenwood [6], pp. 75–6.

(b) I think sometimes our difficulties with our friends abroad result from our natural good manners and reticence. We are apt not to press our points too strongly in the early stages of a negotiation, and then when a crisis arises and we have to take a definite position we are accused of perfidy. I feel we ought to make it quite clear to our European friends that if Little Europe is formed without a parallel development of a Free Trade Area we shall have to reconsider the whole of our political and economic attitude towards Europe. I doubt if we could remain in NATO. We should certainly put on highly protective tariffs and quotas to counteract what Little Europe was doing to us. In other words, we should not allow ourselves to be destroyed little by little. We should fight back with every weapon in our armoury.

Macmillan to Selwyn Lloyd, 24 June 1958 (PRO T234/203), in Sean Greenwood [6], p. 98.

DOCUMENT 7 THE FIRST APPLICATION

The establishment of the EEC and Euratom threatened to leave Britain politically as well as economically disadvantaged, as document (a) makes clear. On 10 August 1961 the government formally requested negotiations on the terms of British entry. The minister in charge of the negotiations, Edward Heath, made clear his belief that the problems were not insuperable (b). The Labour Party was divided on the subject. Its leader, Hugh Gaitskell, initially appeared to favour British entry, but at the Labour Party conference at Brighton on 3 October 1962 he came down decisively against entry on any terms which then seemed likely (c). However, it was not domestic opposition which scuppered British entry, but an effective French veto, delivered by de Gaulle at a press conference on 14 January 1963 (d).

(a) The economic division of Europe will confront the United Kingdom with a most serious situation. There are significant political dangers which Ministers have emphasised in recent months – the fear that, despite the manifest advantages of the rapprochement between France and Germany, economic divisions may weaken the political division of the West at a time when a common Western front is more than ever necessary. If, as seems to be the intention, the policy of the Six is to press forward with economic integration, impetus will be given to political integration. The community may well emerge as a Power comparable in size and influence to the United States and the USSR. The pull of this new power bloc would be bound to dilute our influence with the rest of the world, including the Commonwealth. We should find ourselves replaced as the second member of the North Atlantic Alliance and our relative influence with the United States in all fields would diminish. All this would add to the strains on EFTA. The independence which we have sought to preserve by remaining aloof from European integration would be of doubtful value, since our diminished status would suggest only a minor role for us in international affairs.

Report of the European Economic Association Committee of the Cabinet, 25 May 1960 (PRO CAB 134/1820, EQ(60)27), in Sean Greenwood [6], p. 119.

(b) HM Government are ready to subscribe fully to the aims which you have set yourselves. In particular, we accept without qualification the objectives laid down in Articles 2 and 3 of the Treaty of Rome, including the elimination of internal tariffs, a common customs tariff, a common commercial policy, and a common agricultural policy. We are ready to accept, and to play our full part in, the institutions established under Article 4 and other articles of the Treaty. ...

It would be a tragedy if our entry into the Community forced other members of the Commonwealth to change their whole pattern of trade and consequently, perhaps, their political orientation. I do not think that such a development would be in your interest any more than in ours. ... I turn to the question of UK agriculture. ... Provided we can see that in future – with the new methods decided upon – we are able to maintain the stability and living standards that we have established for our farmers, I believe that the problems raised by the differences in our present methods are in no way insuperable. ... I should next like to consider the position of the countries associated with the UK in the European Free Trade Association. It has long been our view that the present division of Western Europe into two economic groups – a division which in our opinion has political as well as economic dangers – should be brought to an end. ... As you will know from the statement issued by the EFTA Council on July 31, we concluded that each member of EFTA should examine the possibility of entering into a direct relationship with the Community. ...

The United Kingdom and the European Economic Community: Text of a Statement by the Lord Privy Seal at a Meeting with Ministers of Member States of the EEC, Paris, 10 October 1961, Cmnd 1565, HMSO, November 1961.

(c) We must be clear about this: it does mean, if this is the idea, the end of Britain as an independent European state. I make no apology for repeating it. It means the end of a thousand years of history. ... And it does mean the end of the Commonwealth. How can one seriously suppose that if the mother country, the centre of the Commonwealth, is a province of Europe (which is what Federation means) it could continue to exist as the mother country of a series of independent nations? ... If we carry the Commonwealth with us, safeguarded, flourishing, prosperous, if we could safeguard our agriculture, and our EFTA friends were all in it, if we were secure in our employment policy, and if we were able to maintain our independent foreign policy and yet have this wider looser association with Europe, it would indeed be a great ideal. But if this should not prove to be possible; if the Six will not give it to us; if the British Government will not even ask for it, then we must stand firm by what we believe, for the sake of Britain and the world.

Labour Party Annual Conference Report, 1962, p. 155.

(**d**) The Treaty of Rome was concluded between six continental states – states which are, economically speaking, one may say, of the same nature. Indeed, whether it be a matter of their industrial or agricultural production, their external exchanges, their habits or their commercial clientele, their living or working conditions, there is between them much more resemblance than difference. Moreover, they are adjacent, they inter-penetrate, they are an extension of each other through their communications. ... Thereupon Great Britain posed her candidature to the Common Market. She did it after having earlier refused to participate in the Communities which we were building, as well as after creating a sort of Free Trade Area with six other states, and finally ... after having put some pressure on the Six to prevent a real beginning being made in the application of the Common Market.

England thus asked in turn to enter, but on her own conditions. This poses without doubt to each of the six states, and poses to England, problems of a very great dimension. England in effect is insular, she is maritime, she is linked through her exchanges, her markets, her supply lines to the most diverse and often the most distant countries; she pursues essentially industrial and commercial activities, and only slight agricultural ones. She has in all her doings very marked and very original habits and traditions. In short, the nature, the structure, the very situation that are England's differ profoundly from those of the continentals. ...

Frances Nicholson and Roger East [7], pp. 30–1.

DOCUMENT 8   **THE SECOND APPLICATION**

Harold Wilson came to power in 1964 as a noted anti-Marketeer. The extent of Britain's economic problems soon convinced him of the need to seek British membership. Nevertheless, he had to tread carefully, given the degree of opposition within his party. In a speech delivered towards the end of 1966 (a), Wilson attempted to shift the goalposts by arguing that the Communities had themselves changed. De Gaulle's continuing opposition is made clear in document (b), from a press conference at the Elysée palace on 27 November 1967.

(a) Britain has much to give but also much to gain, provided our essential interests can be met, as those of the Common Market countries were met nine years ago. To join the EEC means joining the European Coal and Steel Community and Euratom, and few countries have more to contribute in the fields covered by these communities. In particular, Britain leads the world, barring none, in the peaceful application of atomic energy. ...

I hope that we are not, at every stage in the debates within this country on the government's decision, going to be dominated by the failures of the past. Many of the anxieties that some of us expressed three or four years ago are much less real because of developments within the Common Market and within EFTA. ...

There is no future for Britain in a Little England philosophy. There is no future, either, for anyone in a Little Europe philosophy. For we do not see this venture, any more than our friends in Europe do, as a self-sufficient rich man's club – the identification of the EEC with the development of so many African territories is a manifestation of this, as is the aid the countries of the EEC have given on a wider scale.

Harold Wilson at the Lord Mayor's banquet, Guildhall, 14 November 1966, in Frances Nicholson and Roger East [7], pp. 43–4.

(b) The British people can no doubt see more and more clearly that the structures and customs of its activities, and even its national personality, are from now on put in jeopardy in the great movement which is sweeping the world. ... After all, the serious economic, financial, monetary, and social difficulties with which Britain is grappling make her feel this day after day. From all this emerges a tendency to look for a framework, even a European one, which would help her to save and safeguard her own substance, allow her to play a leading role again, and relieve her of part of her burden. ...

In these conditions, what could be the result of what is called the entry of Britain into the Common Market? If one wished, in spite of everything, to impose it, it would obviously mean the breaking up of a Community which has been built and which functions according to rules which could not bear such a monumental exception. Moreover, this Community would not bear the introduction among its principal members of a state which, precisely because of its currency, its economy, and its politics, is not at present a part of Europe as we have begun to build it. ... In order that the British Isles can really make fast to the Continent, there is still a very vast and deep mutation to be effected.

Frances Nicholson and Roger East [7], pp. 53–5.

DOCUMENT 9   THE THIRD APPLICATION

*De Gaulle's resignation in April 1969 cleared the way for a third British
application. Wilson agreed to enter negotiations but, mindful of Labour
Party divisions, he avoided any premature commitment (a). By the time
negotiations began, Wilson had been replaced by Heath, who had no such
inhibitions. The government White Paper recommending entry painted a
rosy picture of the Community and of Britain's prospects through
membership (b). Wilson eventually came down against membership (c), but
in the crucial Commons vote 69 Labour MPs voted for entry, and a further
20 abstained. On 22 January 1972, Heath signed the Treaty of Accession at
Egmont palace, Brussels, taking the opportunity to outline his vision of a
'new and greater united Europe' (d).*

(a) The question of entry, what I have called the final decision, does not
arise on this White Paper, nor indeed in the debate which will follow. It is
in the light of the negotiations which are due to begin in the near future
that this decision must be taken. The Government and the House, of course,
will recognise that political as well as economic factors are involved. If,
when the decision is to be taken, the disadvantages for Britain appear
excessive in relation to the benefits ... the Government clearly would not
propose to Parliament that we should enter the Communities. If, on the
other hand, the costs, after negotiations, appear acceptable in relation to the
benefits, the Government will recommend entry.

The Government will enter into negotiations resolutely, in good faith,
mindful both of British interests and of the advantages of success in the
negotiations to all the members of an enlarged community.

Parliamentary Debates (Hansard), House of Commons, 5th Series, Vol.
795, 10 February 1970, cols 1083–4.

(b) The Community is no federation of provinces or counties. It constitutes
a Community of great and established nations, each with its own
personality and traditions. The practical working of the Community
accordingly reflects the reality that sovereign Governments are represented
round the table. On a question where a government considers that vital
national interests are involved, it is established that the decision should be
unanimous. Like any other treaty, the Treaty of Rome commits its
signatories to support agreed aims; but the commitment represents the
voluntary undertaking of a sovereign state to observe policies which it has
helped to form. There is no question of any erosion of essential national
sovereignty. ...

The Government is confident that membership of the enlarged
Community will lead to much improved efficiency and productivity in
British industry, with a higher rate of investment and faster growth of real
wages. ... A more efficient United Kingdom industry will be more

competitive not only within the enlarged Community but also in world markets generally. ... The improvement in efficiency will also result in a higher rate of growth in the economy. This will make it possible to provide for a more rapid improvement in our national standard of living as well as pay for the costs of entry.

The United Kingdom and the European Communities, Cmnd 4715, HMSO, July 1971.

(c) The condemnation of this Government is not that they failed to secure terms which would have ensured that the Labour Government's stated requirements were met. The condemnation of them is that they did not even try. ...

I believe that the terms so frivolously negotiated by the right hon. and learned Gentleman inevitably ... involve an intolerable and disproportionate burden on every family in the land and, equally, on Britain's balance of payments. ... The EEC, as it stands today, was recently described in a pro-Market Sunday paper as a Monopolies Commission writ large. That is not true. It is a Monopolies Commission writ large on which there has been superimposed a gigantic public assistance committee, handing out doles without any means test to European farmers.

Parliamentary Debates (Hansard), House of Commons, 5th Series, Vol. 823, 28 October 1971, cols 2080–2102.

(d) Clear thinking will be needed to recognize that each of us within the Community will remain proudly attached to our national identity and to the achievements of our national history and tradition. But at the same time, as the enlargement of the Community makes clear beyond doubt, we have all come to recognize our common European heritage, our mutual interests and our European destiny. ...

What design should we seek for the new Europe? It must be a Europe which is strong and confident within itself. A Europe in which we shall be working for the progressive relaxation and elimination of East-West tensions. A Europe conscious of the interests of its friends and partners. A Europe alive to its great responsibilities in the common struggle of humanity for a better life.

Thus this ceremony marks an end and a beginning. An end to divisions which have stricken Europe for centuries. A beginning of another stage in the construction of a new and greater united Europe. This is the task for our generation in Europe.

Frances Nicholson and Roger East [7], pp. 74–5.

DOCUMENT 10   RENEGOTIATION

*By the time Labour returned to power in 1974, Wilson had patched
together a compromise on the EEC issue: renegotiation of the terms of
entry, followed by a referendum on British membership. The renegotiations
were conducted by James Callaghan, who outlined Britain's grievances in a
speech to the EC Council of Ministers on 1 April 1974 (a). One of his
Cabinet colleagues, Barbara Castle, suspected that Callaghan was not
pursuing the renegotiations with the greatest vigour, a suspicion reinforced
by a Cabinet discussion on 21 November (b).*

(a) In view of the great importance of the issue of membership of the
Community, my government is now engaged in a root and branch review of
the effect of Community policies. ... In particular, we are examining with
great care the working of the common agricultural policy; the estimates for
future contributions to and receipts from the Community budget; the
Community's trade and aid policies towards the Commonwealth and
developing countries; and how far in practice the existing rules, as they are
interpreted, interfere with the powers over the British economy which we
need to pursue effective regional, industrial and fiscal policies. ...

We are not asking for charity. We seek a fair deal. In 1973, only paying
8 per cent of the Community budget in accordance with the transitional
key, we were already the second largest net contributors. At the end of our
normal transitional period we shall be paying over 19 per cent, well over the
16½ per cent which is our likely share of [gross national product] at that
time.

If the full 'own resources' system were to be applied to us with no
changes in 1980, we should find ourselves paying still more, perhaps several
percentage points more, of the Community budget – in even sharper
contrast with the relatively low share of GNP we can then expect to have. ...

Frances Nicholson and Roger East [7], pp. 166–7.

(b) I am now convinced that Jim [Callaghan] is heading for a patch-up deal
to stay in – and is actively pursuing it. I said his speech had alarmed me
more than anything else. We had made no inroads at all on the CAP. The
Community remained as opposed as ever to deficiency payments. All we
had been allowed was 'a little private sin provided we paid for it'. 'Don't
you want to amend the CAP?' snapped Jim. 'I want to abolish it', I retorted.
Otherwise we should be saddled with all its disadvantages and would have
to pay for any improvements we made to it through our own help to
farmers. I warned that the real crunch was still to come and we had better
not live in a fool's paradise. ... Afterwards, as I sat next to Peter [Shore] on
the front bench, he said gloomily that he didn't like the way things were
shaping at all.

Barbara Castle [149], pp. 229–30 (21 November 1974).

DOCUMENT 11   **THE 1975 REFERENDUM**

The renegotiations ended on 11 March 1975. A week later, with the referendum set for 5 June, a majority of the Cabinet decided to endorse continued British membership, on the renegotiated terms. The government's pamphlet (a) was delivered to every house in Britain, together with two others (one for, one against). One of the most powerful sources of opposition to government policy was the TUC (b). By contrast, the new Conservative leader, Margaret Thatcher, was a strong supporter of the 'Yes' campaign (c). The result was a convincing 64.5% in favour of membership (d).

(a) Let us be clear about one thing: In or out of the Common Market, it will be tough going for Britain over the next few years.

In or out, we would still have been hit by the oil crisis, by rocketing world prices for food and raw materials.

But we will be in a much stronger position to face the future if we stay inside the Market than if we try to go it alone.

Inside, on the improved terms, we remain part of the world's most powerful trade bloc. We can help to fix the terms of world trade.

Inside, we can count on more secure supplies of food if world harvests turn out to be bad. And we can help to hold down Market food prices – as we have done since we joined in 1973.

Inside the Market we can work to get more European Community money spent in Britain. ...

Outside, we are on our own. ...

The Government have made THEIR choice. They believe that the new terms of membership are good enough for us to carry on INSIDE the Community. Their advice is to vote for staying in.

Her Majesty's Government, *Britain's New Deal in Europe*, May 1975.

(b) The trade union movement is against Britain staying in the Common Market. The terms of continuing our membership are damaging to the economy, damaging to industry, and damaging to our democratic freedoms. ... In this year's renegotiations, not enough has been done, not enough has been achieved. ...

Being in the Market means that Britain has to pay more – much more – than its fair share of the Common Market budget. ...

Being in the Common Market means throwing away a fair and healthy agricultural system – of low food prices and subsidies to farmers – for one based on high prices and free competition. ...

Being in the Common Market means that the British people no longer have the final say in the way their country is run. Democracy in Britain has been based for centuries on the supreme power of an elected Parliament to pass laws and levy taxes. But this has all been brought into question in the

Common Market. Regulations made in Brussels are law in Britain, and they have to be enforced by our courts and put into effect by our administration. But they are not made by the British people, and they are not made by the British Parliament.

Information broadsheet issued by the Trades Union Congress, May 1975.

(c) First, I believe the Common Market makes a constructive contribution to the peace and security of Europe. ... Today, European peace is taken for granted. But human nature has not changed. It is still possible for a nation to be subjugated by a dominant, determined minority, bent on extinguishing the flame of freedom, in the name of some false but plausible slogan. Prevention lies not only in the willingness of peoples to be vigilant in defence against tyranny; it consists of being prepared to live our lives together, in their becoming so enmeshed through trade and co-operation that to turn on one another would be unthinkable and impossible. ...

Second, our standard of living, and jobs, depend on our ability to produce goods people want at a price they are prepared to pay, and to sell them in the international market place. ... By being in Europe, we gain access to a tariff-free market of 250 million people. ...

Third, the debate has raged fiercely over food prices and supplies. ... In future sometimes we shall pay less in the Community, and sometimes we shall pay more. But we shall have a stable source of supply, and I believe that most housewives would rather pay a little more than risk a bare cupboard. ...

Fourth, Britain has always been involved in world affairs. ... One after another our Commonwealth partners have said they want us to stay in Europe, because it is in their interest that we do so. ...

Fifth, in politics we always have to consider 'what is the alternative?'. ... If we came out now, we should be denouncing a treaty and cold-shouldering our friends. At that precise moment we should have to say: 'Now we have broken one treaty, we want you to give us another on a different basis – as a free trade area'. Such a course of action would deal Britain's reputation a severe blow.

Margaret Thatcher, 'Europe: the choice before us', *Daily Telegraph*, 4 June 1975.

(d) The Result:

'Do you think that the United Kingdom should stay in the European Community (the Common Market)?'

	Total electorate[1]	Total votes[2]	Turnout[1] %	'Yes'[2] %	Highest 'yes'	Lowest 'yes'
England	33,339,959	21,722,222	64.6	68.7	76.3	62.9
Wales	2,015,766	1,345,545	66.7	64.8	74.3	56.9
Scotland	3,698,462	2,286,676	61.7	58.4	72.3	29.5
N. Ireland[2]	1,032,490	498,751	47.4	52.1		
U.K.[1]	40,086,677	26,223,394	64.5	64.5	76.3	29.5

[1] Electorate and turnout figures are for the civilian electorate only. The 370,000 service votes are only in the total votes and in the 'yes' percentages.
[2] The votes were counted on a county basis, except in Northern Ireland which was treated as a single unit. In 66 of the 68 counties there was a 'yes' majority. (Shetland voted 56.3% 'No' and Western Isles 70.5% 'No'.)

David Butler and Gareth Butler [4], p. 220 (amended).

DOCUMENT 12   **THE BRITISH BUDGET QUESTION**

The renegotiations of 1974–75 did little to solve the problem of the excess of British payments to the EC compared to receipts, and by 1979 the problem was becoming acute. Margaret Thatcher set about tackling the issue with vigour, much to the satisfaction of her supporters. Roy Jenkins, who was President of the Commission, believed that Thatcher's style did not help her case (a). A short-term solution was agreed in May 1980, and a longer-term solution in June 1984. Nevertheless, the excess continued to grow, reaching alarming proportions by the late 1980s (b).

(a) The Council started at 3.40. ... There was a certain amount of routine stuff ... first, which lasted longer than I expected (some, I think, were rather keen that it should do so). Then into the budget question about 6 o'clock, introduced briefly by me. Mrs. Thatcher did quite well for once, a bit shrill as usual, but not excessively so. There was quite a good initial response. ... Then towards the end Mrs. Thatcher got the question bogged down by being far too demanding. Her mistake, which fed on itself subsequently at dinner and indeed the next morning, arose out of her having only one of the three necessary qualities of a great advocate. She has nerve and determination to win, but she certainly does not have a good understanding of the case against her (which was based on the own-resources theory, or theology if you like), which means that the constantly reiterated cry of 'It's my money I want back', strikes an insistently jarring note. ... She also lacks the third quality, which is that of not boring the judge or the jury, and she bored everybody endlessly by only understanding about four of the fourteen or so points on the British side and repeating each of them twenty-seven times.

Roy Jenkins, *European Diary*, 1977–81, Collins, London, 1989, pp. 528–9 (29 November 1979).

(b) Net U.K. Payments to European Community institutions (£):[1]

UK Financial Year	Gross Payments	Public Sector Receipts	Negotiated Refunds and Abatements	Total Net Payments
1973–74	200	104	—	96
1974–75	197	232	—	- 35
1975–76	370	354	—	16
1976–77	544	320	—	244
1977–78	941	382	—	540
1978–79	1323	555	—	743
1979–80	1665	781	—	837
1980–81	1900	1022	645	168
1981–82	2330	1161	959	103
1982–83	2820	1323	774	576
1983–84	3097	1885	239	853
1984–85	3614	1892	589	977
1985–86	3745	1930	823	819
1986–87	5121	2557	1343	1074
1987–88	4906	1958	1137	1661
1988–89	5167	2400	1600	1006
1989–90	5804	2035	1317	2316
1990–91	6411	2388	1838	2027
1991–92	6129	2757	2428	705
1992–93	6970	2810	1993	1898
1993–94	8961	4295	2500	1778

[1] Net payments actually made during UK financial years, regardless of the Community budget to which they relate or from which they are financed. From 1978–79 onwards the net payments column excludes the U.K.'s contribution to multilateral overseas aid.

David Butler and Gareth Butler [4], p. 475.

DOCUMENT 13   **THE SINGLE MARKET**

In this extract from her memoirs, Thatcher explains her support for the proposal to complete the single market, which was pushed through largely on the initiative of a British Commissioner, Lord Cockfield. As she makes clear, she accepted the corollary – a significant increase in the powers of the EC institutions, agreed as part of the Single European Act in December 1985.

I had one overriding positive goal. This was to create a single Common Market. The Community's internal tariffs on goods had been abolished in July 1968. At the same time it had become a customs union, which Britain had fully accepted in July 1977. What remained were the so-called 'non-tariff' barriers. These came in a variety of more or less subtle forms. Different national standards on matters ranging from safety to health, regulations discriminating against foreign products, public procurement policies, delays and overelaborate procedures at customs posts – all these and many others served to frustrate the existence of a real Common Market. British businesses would be among those most likely to benefit from an opening-up of other countries' markets. ... The price we would have to pay to achieve a Single Market with all its economic benefits, though, was more majority voting in the Community. There was no escape from that, because otherwise particular countries would succumb to domestic pressures and prevent the opening up of their markets. It also required more power for the European Commission: but that power must be used in order to create and maintain a Single Market rather than to advance other objectives.

Margaret Thatcher [164], pp. 553–4.

DOCUMENT 14   **THATCHER'S EUROPE**

Thatcher became increasingly disenchanted with the European Community, partly in reaction to the federalist mission of the French socialist President of the Commission, Jacques Delors. In her speech at the College of Europe in Bruges on 20 September 1988, she lambasted the supranational ideal, and called for a looser Europe of nations, firmly anchored in the 'Atlantic Community'.

Willing and active cooperation between independent sovereign states is the best way to build a successful European Community. To try to suppress nationhood and concentrate power at the centre of a European con- glomerate would be highly damaging and would jeopardize the objectives we seek to achieve. Europe will be stronger precisely because it has France as France, Spain as Spain, Britain as Britain, each with its own customs, traditions and identity. It would be folly to try to fit them into some sort of identikit European personality. ...

I am the first to say that on many great issues the countries of Europe should try to speak with a single voice. I want to see us work more closely on the things we can do better together than alone. Europe is stronger when we do so, whether it be in trade, in defence, or in relations with the rest of the world. But working more closely together does not require power to be centralised in Brussels or decisions to be taken by an appointed bureaucracy. ... We have not successfully rolled back the frontiers of the state in Britain, only to see them reimposed at a European level, with a European superstate exercising a new dominance from Brussels. ...

Let us have a Europe which plays its full part in the wider world, which looks outward not inward, and which preserves that Atlantic Community –

that Europe on both sides of the Atlantic – which is our noblest inheritance and our greatest strength.

Brent F. Nelsen and Alexander C.-G. Stubbs (eds), *The European Union: Readings on the Theory and Practice of European Integration,* Lynne Reiner, Boulder, Co, 1994, pp. 45–50.

DOCUMENT 15   EUROPE AND THATCHER'S DOWNFALL

Thatcher's increasingly strident anti-Europeanism was to prove a major cause of her downfall. In document (a), reporting to the House of Commons on the Rome Council, she again makes clear her hostility to the idea of European federation, and accuses the leader of the Labour Party, Neil Kinnock, of wishing to sell out on the issue of a single currency. Thatcher's attitude led to the resignation of Sir Geoffrey Howe, whose eloquent rebuttal of Thatcherite Europhobia (b) led directly to the leadership contest which brought her down.

(a) The President of the Commission, Mr. Delors, said at a press conference the other day that he wanted the European Parliament to be the democratic body of the Community, he wanted the Commission to be the Executive and he wanted the Council of Ministers to be the Senate. No. No. No.

Perhaps the Labour party would give all those things up easily. Perhaps it would agree to a single currency and abolition of the pound sterling. Perhaps, being totally incompetent in monetary matters, it would be only too delighted to hand over full responsibility to a central bank, as it did to the IMF. The fact is that the Labour party has no competence on money and no competence on the economy – so, yes, the right hon. Gentleman would be glad to hand it all over. What is the point of trying to get elected to Parliament only to hand over sterling and the powers of this House to Europe?

Parliamentary Debates (Hansard), Sixth Series, Vol. 178, House of Commons, 30 October 1990, col. 873.

(b) It was the late Lord Stockton, formerly Harold Macmillan, who first put the central point clearly. As long ago as 1962, he argued that we had to place and keep ourselves within the EC. He saw it as essential then, as it is today, not to cut ourselves off from the realities of power; not to retreat into a ghetto of sentimentality about our past and so diminish our own control over our own destiny in the future. ...

There is talk, of course, of a single currency for Europe. I agree that there are many difficulties about the concept – both economic and political. Of course, as I said in my letter of resignation, none of us wants the imposition of a single currency. But that is not the real risk. The 11 others cannot impose their solution on the 12th country against its will, but they can go ahead without us. The risk is not imposition but isolation. The real threat is that of leaving ourselves with no say in the monetary arrangements that the rest of Europe chooses for itself, with Britain once again scrambling to join the club later, after the rules have been set and after the power has been distributed by others to our disadvantage. That would be the worst possible outcome. ...

The tragedy is – and it is for me personally, for my party, for our whole people and for my right hon. Friend herself, a very real tragedy – that the Prime Minister's perceived attitude towards Europe is running increasingly serious risks for the future of our nation. It risks minimising our influence and maximising our chances of being once again shut out.

Parliamentary Debates (Hansard), Sixth Series, Vol. 180, House of Commons, 13 November 1990, cols 463–5.

DOCUMENT 16   THE 'EUROSCEPTICS'

Thatcher's successor, John Major, found it increasingly hard to keep the Conservative Party united on Europe. His troubles only increased after the signing of the Maastricht Treaty. In document (a), a leading 'Eurosceptic' calls for a referendum, which he is convinced will reverse government policy. In document (b), a group of leading businessmen warns of the dangers of 'Euroscepticism', on the eve of the 1997 general election.

(a) I believe that we could resolve all the divisive problems of Maastricht if the government considered their attitude to a referendum. If they were prepared to give the people the right to decide the issue, the long and tedious debates on the treaty could end within a few hours. ... People should then be warned that the Maastricht treaty involves a massive surrender of power to non-elected bodies in Europe. The much publicised 'opt out' on economic and monetary union appears to be no more significant than the freedom we give to the people of Scotland to have their own pound note – however symbolic, its existence does not give the Scots the right to determine their own economic policy. The treaty will also involve considerable additional sums being paid by British taxpayers to the EC. Of course government ministers assured us after the Edinburgh summit in December that the extra costs would be rather small, but the leaders of states like Ireland and Spain were received as national heroes when they returned home to report that billions of ecus would pour into their coffers as a result of Edinburgh.

Letter from Sir Teddy Taylor MP, *The Times*, 11 February 1993.

(b) Sir, the Election approaches and it is vital that everyone recognises the real issues facing Britain on Europe. As business people operating not only in Europe but across the world, we have watched with dismay the spread of extreme Euroscepticism and of the mistaken belief that an arm's length and hostile attitude on Europe is now in the UK's best interests. The reality is quite different. The UK is already part of Europe. Nearly 60 per cent of our visible trade is with members of the European Union and this continues to grow. Our direct investments in other member states now exceed our investments in the US. More than 2,000 continental European companies have invested here, taking advantage of our growing competitive advantages in manufacturing. And our outstanding record in attracting non-EU inward investment is driven by our access to the single market...

These benefits would be put at risk if this country chose the path of isolation: Britain would be a poorer place, with lower investment and higher unemployment. The UK must remain a full and committed member of the club. Of course we will want to argue for change, for an improved focus on the challenges which global competition raises. But we cannot expect our proposals and our criticisms to be taken seriously if we refuse to acknowledge the enormous benefits which we have already gained by being part of Europe.

Letter from Sir Colin Marshall and others, *The Financial Times*, 11 March 1997.

DOCUMENT 17   **LABOUR AND EUROPE**

The Labour Party's eighteen years in opposition were marked by a complete turnaround in its policy towards Europe. In 1983, with Michael Foot as leader, the party promised to take the country out of Europe (a). Neil Kinnock's first manifesto, in 1987, promised to stay in, but betrayed a certain hostility to the Community and its policies (b). In 1992 the party was more enthusiastic, in part reflecting the greater prominence attached to social issues by the evolving Community (c). With Blair as leader, in 1997, the revolution was complete, with the Labour Party able to portray itself as the party of Europe (d).

(a) British withdrawal from the Common Market is the right policy for Britain, to be completed well within the lifetime of the parliament. That is our commitment. But we are also committed to bring about withdrawal in an amicable and orderly way, so that we do not prejudice employment or the prospect of increased political and economic co-operation with the whole of Europe.

Labour Party Manifesto, *New Hope for Britain*, June 1983.

(b) Labour's aim is to work constructively with our EEC partners to promote economic expansion and combat unemployment. However, we will stand up for British interests within the European Community and will seek to put an end to the abuses and scandals of the Common Agricultural Policy. We shall, like other member countries, reject EEC interference with our policy for national recovery and renewal.

Labour Party Manifesto, *Britain Will Win*, June 1987.

(c) The Labour government will promote Britain out of the European second division into which our country has been relegated by the Tories. Our first chance will be the United Kingdom's six-months' presidency of the Community, starting on 1 July. We shall use that presidency to end the Tories' opt-out from the Social Chapter, so that the British people can benefit from European safeguards. ... We shall play an active part in negotiations on Economic and Monetary Union. We shall fight for Britain's interests, working for Europe-wide policies to fight unemployment and to enhance regional and structural industrial policy.

Labour Party Manifesto, *It's Time to Get Britain Working Again*, April 1992.

(d) There are only three options for Britain in Europe. The first is to come out. The second is to stay in, but on the sidelines. The third is to stay in, but in a leading role. An increasing number of Conservatives, overtly or covertly, favour the first. But withdrawal would be disastrous for Britain. It would put millions of jobs at risk. It would dry up inward investment. It would destroy our clout in international trade negotiations. It would relegate Britain from the premier division of nations. The second is exactly where we are today under the Conservatives. ... The third is the path a new Labour government will take. A fresh start in Europe, with the credibility to achieve reform. We have set out a detailed agenda for reform, leading from the front during the UK presidency in the first half of 1998.

Labour Party Manifesto, *Because Britain Deserves Better*, May 1997.

DOCUMENT 18   **THE AMSTERDAM COUNCIL**

The Labour Party came to power in 1997 committed to pursuing a positive approach to Europe. The Prime Minister, Tony Blair, claimed to have put Britain's relations with its partners onto a new and more constructive footing after the Amsterdam Council of June 1997. Nevertheless, his emphasis on defending British interests and his choice of policy objectives, including the completion of the single market, illustrated the extent of continuity between Thatcherite Conservatism and Blairite 'New Labour'.

Our aims in the negotiations were to protect our essential interests over immigration, foreign policy, defence and a central role for Britain in Europe, to promote changes of real interest to the British people and to move Europe on to a new and positive agenda. We also promised to bring a fresh and constructive approach to Europe and to the negotiations.

I am happy to tell the house that those objectives have been fully achieved – and they were achieved while at the same time improving both our standing in Europe and our relationships with our European partners.

First, we have obtained legal security for our frontier controls, through a legally binding protocol to the treaty. ... We have also ensured continued protection for our essential interests in all the areas in which we sought it. We have maintained, as we said we would, the veto on matters of foreign policy, defence, treaty change, community finances and tax. We have prevented the extension of qualified majority voting in areas where it might cause damage. ... We have also ruled out other potentially damaging proposals. For example, others wanted to give the European Union explicit legal personality across all the pillars of the treaty. At our instance, that was removed. ...

Second, for the first time in a decade Britain is setting a positive agenda for Europe. In April, I set out in Manchester our platform for reform: completion of the single market, a new emphasis on flexible labour markets and education and skills, reform of wasteful policies in agriculture and elsewhere, enlargement and a more effective common foreign and security policy. Each of those elements was fully reflected at Amsterdam, in the intergovernmental conference or the Council conclusions.

Parliamentary Debates (Hansard), 6th Series, Vol. 296, 18 June 1997, cols 313–14.

DOCUMENT 19   DIRECT ELECTIONS TO THE EUROPEAN PARLIAMENT

Until 1979 members of the European Parliament were nominated, in proportion to the distribution of seats in national parliaments. The agreement to introduce direct elections was signed on 13 July 1976, although it wasn't until June 1979 that the first elections took place. Most analysts agree that the European elections have tended to turn on domestic rather than European issues. The main features of the results since 1979 have been the low turnout, and the steady erosion of support for the Conservatives.

	1979 Thu. 7 June	1984 Thu. 7 June	1989 Thu. 15 June	1994 Thu. 9 June
Electorate	41,152,763	42,493,274	43,180,720	43,037,821
Votes Cast	13,446,083	13,998,274	15,893,408	15,847,417
Turnout (%)	32.7	32.6	36.8	36.8
% Votes				
Con.	48.4	39.9	33.5	26.9
Lab.	31.6	36.0	38.7	42.6
Lib./All	12.6	19.1	6.2	16.1
Nat.[1]	2.5	2.4	3.2	4.1
Other[2]	4.9	5.6	2.8	10.2
Seats				
Con.	60	45	32	18
Lab.	17	32	45	62
Lib./All.	–	–	–	2
Nat.[1]	1	1	–	2
Other[2]	3	3	4	3

[1] Excludes N. Ireland parties
[2] Includes N. Ireland parties.

David Butler and Gareth Butler [4], pp. 220–1 (amended).

CHRONOLOGY

16 June 1940	Declaration of Anglo-French Union
5 July 1945	Labour election victory: Attlee becomes Prime Minister on 26 July
19 Sept. 1946	Churchill's Zürich speech calling for a 'United States of Europe'
5 June 1947	Marshall proposes US aid to Europe
29 Oct. 1947	Creation of Benelux
17 Mar. 1948	Brussels Treaty: British guarantee defence of western Europe
16 April 1948	OEEC formed
7 May 1948	Hague Congress: call for a Council of Europe
4 April 1949	Treaty of Washington, establishing NATO
5 May 1949	Statute of Council of Europe
23 Feb. 1950	Labour narrowly win election
9 May 1950	Schuman Plan for an ECSC
24 Oct. 1950	Pleven Plan for an EDC
18 April 1951	Treaty of Paris, establishing ECSC
25 Oct. 1951	Conservative election victory: Churchill replaces Attlee
27 May 1952	Treaty to create EDC
30 Aug. 1954	EDC rejected by French National Assembly
23 Oct. 1954	Treaty creating WEU
6 April 1955	Eden replaces Churchill as Prime Minister
25 May 1955	Conservative election victory
1–3 June 1955	Messina Conference: 'the Six' agree further integration
10 Jan. 1957	Macmillan replaces Eden as Prime Minister
25 Mar. 1957	Treaties of Rome, establishing EEC and Euratom
1 Jan. 1958	Rome Treaties come into force
8 Oct. 1959	Conservative election victory
20 Nov 1959	EFTA established by 'the Seven'
10 Aug. 1961	Britain requests negotiations aiming at membership of EC
8 Nov. 1961	British negotiations open in Brussels
14 Jan. 1962	EEC agrees Common Agricultural Policy
14 Jan. 1963	De Gaulle vetoes British application
29 Jan. 1963	British negotiations with EC broken off
1 July 1963	First Yaoundé Convention
18 Oct. 1963	Douglas-Home replaces Macmillan as Prime Minister

15 Oct. 1964	Labour narrowly wins election: Wilson becomes Prime Minister
1 July 1965	French begin boycott of EC institutions
29 Jan. 1966	Luxembourg compromise
31 Mar. 1966	Labour election victory
10 Nov. 1966	Wilson announces intention to seek membership of EC
1 Jan. 1967	Merger of the three Communities
11 May 1967	Britain applies for membership of EC
27 Nov. 1967	De Gaulle announces continuing opposition to British entry
16 May 1968	Formal French veto on British application
25 April 1969	De Gaulle resigns as President of France
2 Dec. 1969	Hague Summit: EC agrees to re-open negotiations with Britain
18 June 1970	Conservative election victory: Heath replaces Wilson
30 June 1970	Negotiations resumed in Luxembourg
23 June 1971	Council of Ministers announces agreement with Britain
28 Oct. 1971	Commons endorses membership on terms negotiated
22 Jan. 1972	Treaty of Accession signed by Britain, Denmark, Ireland and Norway
13 July 1972	Commons passes European Communities Bill
22 July 1972	EC signs free trade agreements with remaining EFTA countries
25 Sept. 1972	Referendum in Norway rejects EC membership
1 Jan. 1973	Britain, Denmark and Ireland become members of EC
28 Feb. 1974	Election: Labour largest party: Wilson replaces Heath
1 April 1974	Labour opens renegotiation of British membership
10 Oct. 1974	Election: narrow Labour majority
2 Feb 1975	First Lomé Convention
9 April 1975	Commons endorses renegotiated terms
5 June 1975	Referendum endorses continued British membership of EC
22 July 1975	New budgetary powers for European Parliament
5 April 1976	Callaghan replaces Wilson as Prime Minister
13 July 1976	Agreement on direct elections to European Parliament
31 Dec. 1977	Transitional period for Britain ends
12 Mar. 1979	Start of European Monetary System
3 May 1979	Conservative election victory: Thatcher replaces Callaghan
7 June 1979	First direct elections to European Parliament
2 Dec. 1979	Dublin Council: Britain demands budgetary adjustment
30 May 1980	Short-term solution to budgetary dispute accepted
6 Jan. 1981	Greece joins EC
18 May 1982	British veto on agricultural price increases overruled
9 June 1983	Conservative election victory
14 Feb. 1984	European Parliament adopts draft Treaty of European Union
14 June 1984	Second direct elections to European Parliament

14 June 1984	Commission proposes completion of single market by 31 Dec. 1992
26 June 1984	Fontainebleau Council: longer-term solution of budgetary dispute
3 Dec. 1985	Luxembourg Council agrees Single European Act
1 Jan. 1986	Spain and Portugal join EC
11 June 1987	Conservative election victory
1 July 1987	Single European Act comes into force
20 Sept. 1988	Thatcher's Bruges speech criticising European integration
15 June 1989	Third direct elections to European Parliament
8 Dec. 1989	Strasbourg Council: Britain isolated on Social Charter
3 Oct. 1990	German reunification: East German Länder join EC
8 Oct. 1990	Britain joins ERM
28 Oct. 1990	Rome Council: Britain isolated on monetary union: Howe resigns
28 Nov. 1990	Major replaces Thatcher as Prime Minister
11 Dec. 1991	Maastricht Council: agreement on new Treaty
7 Feb. 1992	Maastricht Treaty
9 April 1992	Conservative election victory
16 Sept. 1992	'Black Wednesday': Britain leaves ERM
4 Nov. 1992	Government narrowly wins Commons vote on Maastricht Bill
22 July 1993	Government loses Commons vote on Social Chapter
1 Nov. 1993	Maastricht Treaty comes into force
9 June 1994	Fourth direct elections to European Parliament
1 Jan. 1995	Austria, Finland and Sweden join EC
8 Dec. 1995	Madrid Council confirms 1999 as start of EMU
29 Mar. 1996	Turin Council: inter-governmental conference to review Maastricht
2 April 1996	Government promises referendum before joining single currency
13 Dec. 1996	Dublin Council: agreement on single currency by 1 Jan. 1999
1 May 1997	Labour election victory: Blair replaces Major
17 June 1997	Amsterdam Council: agreement on new treaty

GLOSSARY

Benelux Belgium, the Netherlands and Luxembourg, linked by a customs union since 1947.

Commission, The Executive body of the EC/EU, formed from the merger of the ECSC High Authority and the EEC and Euratom Commissions in 1967. Responsible both for initiating and for implementing legislative decisions. Consists of twenty Commissioners, nominated by member states. Britain's two Commissioners have invariably been politicians from each of the two main parties. Based in Brussels.

Common Agricultural Policy (CAP) One of the objectives of the Treaties of Rome, creating a managed market for agricultural produce by means of a single internal market, common external tariffs, and a system of market interventions and subsidies to maintain production and stabilise prices. By far the most costly of the EC/EU's policies, and one causing difficulties for other food exporters.

Common Market A free trade area protected by common external tariffs, one of the principal aims of the EEC. Name also widely used to describe the EEC/EC.

Council of Europe Organization founded by Britain and nine other western European states in May 1949, to promote cooperation by non-binding conventions and agreements in such fields as human rights, culture and protection of the environment. Subsequently joined by most other western European states. Consists of a Committee of Foreign Ministers, a Consultative Assembly nominated by member governments, and a Commission and European Court of Human Rights. Based in Strasbourg. Entirely separate from the EC/EU institutions (including the European Council).

Council of Ministers The most powerful of the EC/EU institutions, being the main decision-taking and legislative body. Consists of one minister from each member state, either the foreign minister or the minister responsible for the business in hand (e.g. agriculture, transport or energy). Some decisions require unanimity, others require a 'qualified majority' (i.e. roughly two-thirds of the Council's votes, which are weighted in proportion to population). Under the 'Luxembourg compromise' any state may veto a decision on the grounds of national interest, but the use of 'qualified majority voting' has increased. Presidency rotates amongst member-states every six months. See also European Council.

Economic and Monetary Union (EMU) Proposal to create a single currency backed by a European Central Bank. First agreed at Hague summit in December 1969, but soon abandoned. Agreed by the Maastricht summit in December 1991. Non-compulsory, and may be joined only by member states meeting certain financial and economic criteria. Currently scheduled for inauguration in 1999.

European Atomic Energy Community (Euratom) One of the three European Communities, formed by 'the Six' in 1957 to control the development of nuclear power. Had own Commission, but shared other institutions with the ECSC and EEC. Merged with the other two Communities in 1967.

European Coal and Steel Community (ECSC) The first of the three European Communities, formed by 'the Six' in 1951, establishing a common market in coal, iron, steel and their products. Institutions included a Council of Ministers, a Common Assembly (European Parliament), a European Court of Justice and a High Authority. Merged with the other two Communities in 1967.

European Communities (EC) Collective name for the ECSC, the EEC and Euratom, whose executive bodies merged in 1967. Since then, also known as the European Community. Known as the European Union since 1993.

European Council Since 1975, summit meetings of the heads of state or government of EC/EU member states, meeting as the Council of Ministers. Meetings take place two or three times a year, to decide major policy issues. Presidency rotates, in line with Council of Ministers.

European Court of Human Rights Court set up in 1959 by the Council of Europe, to examine violations of the European Convention on Human Rights, signed in 1950. Decisions are non-binding, but usually complied with. Based in Strasbourg.

European Court of Justice Court established to ensure observance of ECSC/EC/EU legislation (which in certain areas takes precedence over national legislation) and to interpret the fundamental treaties. Consists of one judge from each member state, appointed for six years. Decisions are binding. Based in Luxembourg.

European Currency Unit (Ecu) European currency, based on a currencies 'basket' of the member states. Unit of account for EC/EU institutions, and increasingly used by companies and individuals.

European Defence Community (EDC) Scheme to create a European army, to be controlled by a European Political Community. Accepted by the governments of 'the Six' in May 1952, but rejected by the French National Assembly in August 1954.

European Economic Community (EEC) Most important of the three European Communities, formed by 'the Six' in 1957. Aimed at the gradual realisation of a common market (internal free trade and common external tariffs) and further measures of economic integration, including joint policies to deal with agriculture, transport, regional development and social problems. Shared most institutions with the ECSC, but had its own Commission (less powerful than the ECSC's High Authority). Merged with the ECSC and Euratom in 1967.

European Free Trade Association (EFTA) Alternative to the EEC, established by Britain and six other western European states in 1959. Inaugurated an industrial free trade area, but left agriculture and control of external tariffs to member states. Britain and Denmark left EFTA on joining the EC. The remaining members signed free trade agreements with the EC.

European Monetary System (EMS) System inaugurated in March 1979 to stabilise currency fluctuations, by means of an Exchange Rate Mechanism (ERM) and a European Currency Unit (Ecu) backed by a proportion of member-states' gold and dollar reserves. Britain has been a member of the EMS since its inception, but joined the ERM only between October 1990 and September 1992.

European Parliament The successor to the Common Assembly of the ECSC, initially consisting of delegates from national parliaments, but since 1979 consisting of representatives (MEPs) directly elected every five years by voters in the EC/EU member states. Britain currently elects 87 out of 626 MEPs. Initially purely consultative, but given substantial control over the budget in 1975, and further powers by the Single European Act and the Maastricht Treaty. Based in Strasbourg, with secretariat in Luxembourg.

European Political Community (EPC) Scheme to accompany European army (EDC). Rejected in 1954.

European Regional Development Fund (ERDF) Fund established in 1975 to promote regional development, by means of grants channelled through national governments.

European Union (EU) Name given to the European Communities (EC) since 1 November 1993, following the entry into force of the Maastricht Treaty.

Exchange Rate Mechanism (ERM) Part of the EMS, a mechanism for stabilising exchange rates, by keeping national currencies' exchange values within a small margin on either side of an agreed central rate, based on the Ecu. Central banks are obliged to intervene when a currency reaches its 'floor' or 'ceiling', but central rates can be realigned when necessary.

General Agreement on Tariffs and Trade (GATT) UN agreement for the purpose of liberalising world trade, first signed in 1948, and re-negotiated periodically. The EC/EU is not formally a member, but EC/EU member states are represented by the Commission.

Intergovernmental Conference (IGC) Procedure for agreeing changes to the treaty basis of the EC/EU. Can be initiated by majority vote in the Council of Ministers, under article 236 of the EEC Treaty of Rome.

Lomé Conventions Series of agreements replacing the Yaoundé Conventions, the first signed in 1975, later extended to cover more than sixty African-Caribbean-Pacific countries.

Luxembourg Compromise Agreement of February 1966 whereby any member-state may veto decisions on the grounds of national interest.

Maastricht, Treaty of Treaty signed on 7 February 1992, creating the European Union (EU), and envisaging a common foreign and security policy and increased cooperation in justice and law enforcement. Britain allowed to opt out of monetary union and the Social Chapter.

North Atlantic Treaty Organisation (NATO) Defensive alliance of western European states together with the United States and Canada, established by the Treaty of Washington in April 1949. Most EC/EU states are members of NATO, but France, Ireland and some of the more recent members are not.

Organisation for Economic Co-operation and Development (OECD) Consultative organisation replacing the OEEC from 1961, extended to include the United States, Canada, Australia, New Zealand and Japan.

Organisation for European Economic Co-operation (OEEC) Organisation of western European states formed in 1948, to allocate American 'Marshall Aid' and promote the liberalisation of trade and inter-governmental consultation on economic and monetary policy. Replaced by the OECD in 1961.

Paris, Treaty of Treaty establishing the ECSC, signed by 'the Six' on 18 April 1951.

Pleven Plan Proposal by René Pleven, French Prime Minister, on 24 October 1950, to create a European Defence Community (EDC).

Rome, Treaties of Treaties establishing the EEC and Euratom, signed by 'the Six' on 25 March 1957.

Schuman Plan Plan announced by Robert Schuman, French Foreign Minister, on 9 May 1950, to place French, German and other European coal and steel industries under a common 'High Authority'. Led to the creation of the ECSC.

Single European Act (SEA) Legislation agreed by the European Council in December 1985, signed in February 1986, and implemented from July 1987, extending qualified majority voting in the Council of Ministers, enhancing the role of the European Parliament, and widening the scope of EC activities and responsibilities.

Six, The Belgium, France, Italy, Luxembourg, the Netherlands and West Germany, the original members of the three European Communities (ECSC, EEC and Euratom).

Social Chapter Part of the Treaty of Maastricht, envisaging common policies for the protection of workers. Rejected by Britain's Conservative government, which negotiated an 'opt-out'.

Western European Union (WEU) Defensive alliance created in 1954 by the Brussels Treaty powers (Britain, France and Benelux), together with Italy and West Germany, following the failure of the EDC. The framework for the rearmament of West Germany and its integration into NATO.

Yaoundé Conventions Agreements signed in 1963 and 1969, guaranteeing duty-free or preferential access to the European market for products of ex-dependent African territories signing the Conventions, and providing a common EC/EU overseas aid programme.

MAP

The European Union

Map 131

RUSSIA

FINLAND
1995

ESTONIA
1995

LATVIA
1995

LITHUANIA
1995

BELARUS

UKRAINE

MOLDOVA

ROMANIA
1995

BLACK SEA

BULGARIA
1995

TURKEY

GREECE
198

CYPRUS
1990

0   300 mls

0   400 km

*Eastern Länder joined with German unification in 1990

BIBLIOGRAPHY

The place of publication is London unless otherwise stated.

PRIMARY SOURCES AND DOCUMENTARY COLLECTIONS

1 Bullen, Roger and Margaret Pelly (eds), *Documents on British Policy Overseas*, Series II, Volume I, *The Schuman Plan, The Council of Europe and Western European Integration, 1950–52*, HMSO, 1986.

2 Bullen, Roger and Margaret Pelly (eds), *Documents on British Policy Overseas*, Series II, Volume II, *The London Conferences: Anglo-American Relations and Cold War Strategy: January-June 1950*, HMSO, 1987.

3 Bullen, Roger and Margaret Pelly (eds), *Documents on British Policy Overseas*, Series II, Volume III, *German Rearmament: September-December 1950*, HMSO, 1989.

4 Butler, David and Gareth, *British Political Facts, 1900–1994*, Macmillan, 1994.

5 Butler, Lawrence and Harriet Jones (eds), *Britain in the Twentieth Century: A Documentary Reader*, Vol. II, *1939–70*, Heinemann, Oxford, 1995.

6 Greenwood, Sean (ed.), *Britain and European Integration Since the Second World War*, Manchester University Press, Manchester, 1996.

7 Nicholson, Frances and Roger East, *From the Six to the Twelve: The Enlargement of the European Communities*, Longman, Harlow, 1987.

8 *Parliamentary Debates* (Hansard), House of Commons, Fifth and Sixth Series.

9 Pelly, Margaret, Heather Yasamee and Gillian Bennett (eds), *Documents on British Policy Overseas*, Series I, Volume V, *Germany and Western Europe: 11 August-31 December 1945*, HMSO, 1990.

BRITAIN: GENERAL

10 Childs, David, *Britain Since 1945*, Routledge, 3rd edn, 1992.

11 Darwin, John, *Britain and Decolonisation*, Macmillan, 1988.

12   Holland, Robert, *The Pursuit of Greatness: Britain and the World Role, 1900–1970*, Fontana, 1991.

13   Porter, Bernard, *The Lion's Share: A Short History of British Imperialism, 1850–1983*, Longman, Harlow, 6th edn, 1984.

14   Reynolds, David, *Britannia Overruled*, Longman, Harlow, 1991.

15   Robbins, Keith, *The Eclipse of a Great Power: Modern Britain, 1870–1992*, Longman, Harlow, 2nd edn, 1994.

16   Sanders, David, *Losing an Empire, Finding a Role: British Foreign Policy Since 1945*, Macmillan, 1990.

EUROPE: GENERAL

17   Dedman, Martin, *The Origins and Development of the European Union, 1945–95*, Routledge, 1996.

18   Dinan, Desmond, *Ever Closer Union? An Introduction to the European Community*, Macmillan, 1994.

19   Duchêne, François, *Jean Monnet: The First Statesman of Interdependence*, W.W. Norton, 1994.

20   Milward, Alan, *The European Rescue of the Nation State*, Routledge, 1992.

21   Monnet, Jean, *Memoirs*, Collins, 1978.

22   Pinder, John, *European Community: The Building of a Union*, Oxford University Press, Oxford, 2nd edn, 1995.

23   Pryce, Roy, *The Politics of the European Community*, Butterworth, 1973.

24   Stevens, Christopher, *The EEC and the Third World*, Hodder and Stoughton, 1981.

25   Wallace, William, *The Transformation of Western Europe*, Pinter, 1990.

26   Wallace, William, *The Dynamics of European Integration*, Pinter, 1992.

BRITAIN AND EUROPE: GENERAL

27   Bailey, Richard, *The European Connection: Implications of EEC Membership*, Pergamon Press, Oxford, 1983.

28   Barker, Elizabeth, *Britain in a Divided Europe, 1945–70*, Weidenfeld and Nicolson, 1971.

29   Barnet, J.R., *Allies: America, Europe and Japan Since the War*, Cape, 1984.

30   Bell, P.M.H., *France and Britain, 1940–94: The Long Separation*, Longman, Harlow, 1997.

31   Beloff, Lord, *Britain and European Union: Dialogue of the Deaf*, Macmillan, 1996.

32   Brivati, Brian and Harriet Jones (eds), *From Reconstruction to Integration: Britain and Europe Since 1945*, Leicester University Press, Leicester, 1993.

33   Bulmer, Simon, Stephen George and Andrew Scott (eds), *The United Kingdom and EC Membership Evaluated*, Pinter, 1992.

34   Charlton, Michael, *The Price of Victory*, BBC, 1983.

35   Denman, Roy, *Missed Chances: Britain and Europe in the Twentieth Century*, Cassell, 1996.

36   George, Stephen, *An Awkward Partner: Britain in the European Community*, Oxford University Press, Oxford, 2nd edn, 1994.

37   George, Stephen, *Britain and European Integration Since 1945*, Blackwell, Oxford, 1991.

38   Greenwood, Sean, *Britain and European Cooperation Since 1945*, Blackwell, Oxford, 1992.

39   Howe, Sir Geoffrey, 'Sovereignty and interdependence: Britain's place in the world', *International Affairs*, 66/4, October 1990.

40   Jenkins, Roy, *A Life at the Centre*, Macmillan, 1991.

41   Lieber, Robert J., *British Politics and European Unity: Parties, Elites and Pressure Groups*, University of California Press, Berkeley, Cal, 1970.

42   Manderson-Jones, R.B., *The Special Relationship: Anglo-American Relations and Western European Unity, 1947–56*, Weidenfeld and Nicolson, 1972.

43   Nutting, Anthony, *Europe Will Not Wait*, Hollis and Carter, 1961.

44   Wallace, William, 'What price independence? Sovereignty and independence in British politics', *International Affairs*, 62/3, 1986.

45   Young, John W., *Britain and European Unity, 1945–92*, Macmillan, 1993.

BEFORE 1945

46   Bell, P., 'Discussion of European Integration in Britain, 1942–45', in Walter Lipgens (ed.), *Documents on the History of European Integration*, Vol. 2, Walter de Gruyter, Berlin and New York, 1986.

47   Black, Jeremy, *Convergence or Divergence? Britain and the Continent*, Macmillan, 1994.

48   Bosco, Andrea, *Federal Union and the Origins of the 'Churchill Proposal'*, Lothian Foundation Press, 1992.

49   Boyce, Robert, *British Capitalism at the Crossroads, 1919–32*, Cambridge University Press, Cambridge, 1987.

50   Boyce, Robert, 'British capitalism and the idea of European unity between the wars', in P.M.R. Stirk (ed.), *European Unity in Context: The Interwar Period*, Pinter, 1989.

51 Boyce, Robert, 'Was there a "British" alternative to the Briand Plan?', in Peter Catterall and C.J. Morris (eds), *Britain and the Threat to Stability in Europe, 1918–45*, Leicester University Press, Leicester, 1993.

52 Colley, Linda, *Britons: Forging the Nation, 1707–1837*, Yale University Press, 1992.

53 Darwin, John, 'Imperialism in decline?', *Historical Journal*, 23/3, 1980.

54 Gallagher, John, *The Decline, Revival and Fall of the British Empire*, Cambridge University Press, Cambridge, 1982.

55 Howard, Michael, *The Continental Commitment: The Dilemma of British Defence Policy in the Era of Two World Wars*, Penguin edn, Harmondsworth, 1974.

56 Macfarlane, Alan, *The Origins of English Individualism*, Blackwell, Oxford, 1978.

57 Mayne, Richard, John Pinder and John C. de V. Roberts, *Federal Union: The Pioneers*, Macmillan, 1990.

58 Shlaim, Avi, *Britain and the Origins of European Unity, 1940–51*, University of Reading Press, Reading, 1978.

59 White, Ralph, 'The British response to the Briand Plan', in A. Bosco (ed.), *The Federal Idea*, Vol. 1, Lothian Foundation Press, 1991.

60 Woodward, Sir Llewellyn and M.E. Lambert, *British Foreign Policy in the Second World War*, Vol. V, HMSO, 1976.

LABOUR'S EUROPE, 1945–51

61 Acheson, Dean, *Present at the Creation: My Years in the State Department*, Norton, New York, 1969.

62 Adamthwaite, Anthony, 'Britain and the world, 1948–49: the view from the Foreign Office', *International Affairs*, 61/2, 1985.

63 Baylis, John, *The Diplomacy of Pragmatism: Britain and the Formation of NATO, 1942–49*, Macmillan, 1993.

64 Bullock, Alan, *Ernest Bevin: Foreign Secretary*, Heinemann, 1983.

65 Croft, Stuart, 'British policy towards western Europe, 1945–51', in Peter M.R. Stirk and David Willis (eds), *Shaping Postwar Europe: European Unity and Disunity, 1945–57*, Pinter, 1991.

66 Deighton, Anne, 'Britain and the three interlocking circles', in Antonio Varsori (ed.), *Europe, 1945–1990s: The End of an Era?*, Macmillan, 1995.

67 Donoughue, Bernard and G.W. Jones, *Herbert Morrison: Portrait of a Politician*, 1993.

68 Edmonds, Robin, *Setting the Mould: The United States and Britain, 1945–50*, Oxford University Press, Oxford, 1986.

69 Ellwood, David W., *Rebuilding Europe: Western Europe, America and Postwar Reconstruction*, Longman, Harlow, 1992.

70   Greenwood, Sean, 'Ernest Bevin, France and "Western Union",
      August 1945–February 1946', *European History Quarterly*, 14/3,
      1984.
71   Hennessy, Peter, *Never Again: Britain, 1945–51*, Jonathan Cape,
      1992.
72   Hogan, Michael J., *The Marshall Plan: America, Britain and the
      Reconstruction of Western Europe, 1947–52*, Cambridge University
      Press, Cambridge, 1989.
73   Lipgens, Walter, *A History of European Integration, 1945–47: The
      Formation of the European Union*, Clarendon Press, Oxford, 1982.
74   Lord, Christopher, *Absent at the Creation: Britain and the
      Formation of the European Community, 1950–52*, Dartmouth,
      Aldershot, 1996.
75   Milward, Alan, *The Reconstruction of Western Europe, 1945–51*,
      Methuen, 1984.
76   Morgan, Kenneth, *Labour in Power, 1945–51*, Oxford University
      Press, Oxford, 1985.
77   Newton, Scott, 'Britain, the sterling area and European integration,
      1945–50', *Journal of Imperial and Commonwealth History*, 13/3,
      1985.
78   Pelling, Henry, *The Labour Government, 1945–51*, Macmillan,
      1984.
79   Pelling, Henry, *Britain and the Marshall Plan*, Macmillan, 1988.
80   Rothwell, Victor, *Britain and the Cold War, 1941–47*, Cape, 1982.
81   Sahm, Ulrich and Kenneth Younger, 'Britain and Europe, 1950',
      International Affairs, 43/1, 1967.
82   Warner, Geoffrey, 'The Labour governments and the unity of
      western Europe, 1945–51', in Ritchie Ovendale (ed.), *The Foreign
      Policy of the British Labour Governments, 1945–51*, University of
      Leicester Press, Leicester, 1984.
83   Warner, Geoffrey, 'Britain and Europe in 1948: the view from the
      Cabinet', in Josef Becker and Franz Knipping (eds), *Power in
      Europe? Great Britain, France, Italy and Germany in a Post-War
      World, 1945–50*, Walter de Gruyter, Berlin, 1986.
84   Young, John W., *Britain, France and the Unity of Europe, 1945–51*,
      University of Leicester Press, Leicester, 1984.

THE CONSERVATIVES' EUROPE, 1951–57

85   Adamthwaite, Anthony, 'Introduction: the Foreign Office and
      policy-making', in John W. Young (ed.), *The Foreign Policy of
      Churchill's Peacetime Administration, 1951–55*, Leicester University
      Press, Leicester, 1988.
86   Beloff, Max, 'Churchill and Europe', in Robert Blake and Wm. Roger
      Louis (eds), *Churchill*, Oxford University Press, Oxford, 1993.

87   Boothby, Lord, *My Yesterday, Your Tomorrow*, Hutchinson, 1962.

88   Carlton, David, *Anthony Eden*, Allen and Unwin, 1986.

89   Carlton, David, *Britain and the Suez Crisis*, Blackwell, Oxford, 1989.

90   Ceadel, Martin, 'British parties and the European situation, 1950–57', in Ennio di Nolfo (ed.), *Power in Europe? II: Great Britain, France, Germany and Italy, and the Origins of the EEC, 1952–57*, Walter de Gruyter, Berlin, 1992.

91   Fursdon, Edward, *The European Defence Community: A History*, Macmillan, 1980.

92   Gilbert, Martin, *Never Despair: Winston S. Churchill, 1945–65*, Minerva, 1988.

93   Gillingham, John, *Coal, Steel and the Rebirth of Europe, 1945–55*, Cambridge University Press, Cambridge, 1991.

94   Horne, Alistair, *Macmillan*, Vol. 1, *1894–1956*, Macmillan, 1988.

95   Lamb, Richard, *The Failure of the Eden Government*, Sidgwick and Jackson, 1987.

96   Lyon, Peter, 'The Commonwealth and the Suez crisis', in Wm. Roger Louis and Roger Owen (eds), *Suez 1956: The Crisis and its Consequences*, Oxford University Press, Oxford, 1989.

97   Macmillan, Harold, *Tides of Fortune, 1945–55*, Macmillan, 1969.

98   Mager, Olaf, 'Anthony Eden and the framework of security: Britain's alternative to the EDC, 1951–54', in B. Heuser and R. O'Neill (eds), *Securing Peace in Europe, 1945–61*, Macmillan, 1992.

99   Moon, Jeremy, *European Integration in British Politics, 1950–63: A Study of Issue Change*, Gower, Aldershot, 1985.

100 Rhodes James, Robert, *Anthony Eden*, Weidenfeld and Nicolson, 1986.

101 Weigall, David, 'British perceptions of the European Defence Community', in Peter M.R. Stirk and David Willis (eds), *Shaping Postwar Europe: European Unity and Disunity, 1945–57*, Pinter, 1991.

102 Young, John W., 'Churchill's "no" to Europe: the "rejection" of European union by Churchill's post-war government, 1951–52', *Historical Journal*, 28/4, 1985.

103 Young, John W., 'German rearmament and the European Defence Community', in John W. Young (ed.), *The Foreign Policy of Churchill's Peacetime Administration, 1951–55*, Leicester University Press, Leicester, 1988.

104 Young, John W., 'The Schuman Plan and British association', in John W. Young (ed.), *The Foreign Policy of Churchill's Peacetime Administration, 1951–55*, Leicester University Press, Leicester, 1988.

105 Young, John W., '"The parting of the ways?" Britain, the Messina conference and the Spaak committee, June-December 1955' in Michael Dockrill and John W. Young (eds), *British Foreign Policy, 1945–56*, Macmillan, 1989.

MACMILLAN AND THE FIRST APPLICATION, 1957–64

106   Beloff, Nora, *The General Says No: Britain's Exclusion from Europe*, Penguin, Harmondsworth, 1963.

107   Butt, Ronald, 'The Common Market and Conservative Party politics, 1961–62', *Government and Opposition*, 2/3, 1967.

108   Camps, Miriam, *Britain and the European Community, 1955–63*, Oxford University Press, Oxford, 1964.

109   Deighton, Anne, 'The United Kingdom Application for EEC Membership, 1961–63', in Richard Griffiths and Stuart Ward (eds), *Courting the Common Market: The First Attempt to Enlarge the European Community, 1961–63*, Lothian Foundation Press, 1996.

110   Gallup International, 'Public Opinion and the European Community', *Journal of Common Market Studies*, 2/2, 1963.

111   Griffiths, Richard, 'A slow one hundred and eighty degree turn: British policy towards the Common Market, 1955–60', in George Wilkes (ed.), *Britain's Failure to Enter the European Community, 1961–63*, Frank Cass, 1997.

112   Lamb, Richard, *The Macmillan Years, 1957–63: The Emerging Truth*, John Murray, 1995.

113   Lee, Sabine, 'Staying in the game? Coming into the game? Macmillan and European integration', in Richard Aldous and Sabine Lee (eds), *Harold Macmillan and Britain's World Role*, Macmillan, 1996.

114   Ludlow, N. Piers, 'British agriculture and the Brussels negotiations: a problem of trust', in George Wilkes (ed.), *Britain's Failure to Enter the European Community, 1961–63*, Frank Cass, 1997.

115   Macmillan, Harold, *Riding the Storm, 1956–59*, Macmillan, 1971.

116   Macmillan, Harold, *Pointing the Way, 1959–61*, Macmillan, 1972.

117   Macmillan, Harold, *At the End of the Day, 1961–63*, Macmillan, 1973.

118   Turner, John, *Macmillan*, Longman, Harlow, 1994.

119   Ward, Stuart, 'United house or abandoned ship? EFTA and the EEC membership crisis, 1961–63', in Richard Griffiths and Stuart Ward (eds), *Courting the Common Market: The First Attempt to Enlarge the European Community, 1961–63*, Lothian Foundation Press, 1996.

120   Wilkes, George, 'The first failure to steer Britain into the European Communities', in George Wilkes (ed.), *Britain's Failure to Enter the European Community, 1961–63*, Frank Cass, 1997.

121   Williams, Charles, *The Last Great Frenchman: A Life of General de Gaulle*, Little, Brown, 1993.

122   Williams, Philip, *Hugh Gaitskell: A Political Biography*, Jonathan Cape, 1979.

WILSON AND THE SECOND APPLICATION, 1964–70

123 Castle, Barbara, *The Castle Diaries, 1964–70*, Weidenfeld and Nicolson, 1984.

124 Crossman, Richard, *Diaries of a Cabinet Minister, Volume I: Minister of Housing, 1964–66*, Hamilton, 1975.

125 Crossman, Richard, *Diaries of a Cabinet Minister, Volume II: Lord President of the Council and Leader of the House of Commons, 1966–68*, Hamilton, 1976.

126 Durant, Henry, 'Public opinion and the EEC', *Journal of Common Market Studies*, 6/3, 1968.

127 Frey, Cynthia W., 'Meaning business: the British application to join the Common Market, November 1966–October 1967', *Journal of Common Market Studies*, 6/3, 1968.

128 King, Cecil, *The Cecil King Diary, 1965–70*, Jonathan Cape, 1972.

129 Kitzinger, Uwe, *The Second Try: Labour and the EEC*, Pergamon, Oxford, 1968.

130 Morgan, Kenneth O., 'Harold Wilson', in *Labour People*, Oxford University Press, Oxford, 1987.

131 Pimlott, Ben, *Harold Wilson*, Harper and Collins, 1992.

132 Stewart, Michael, *The Jekyll and Hyde Years: Politics and Economic Policy Since 1974*, J.M. Dent, 1977.

133 Wilson, Harold, *The Labour Government, 1964–70: A Personal Record*, Michael Joseph, 1971.

134 Wrigley, Chris, 'Now you see it, now you don't: Harold Wilson and Labour's foreign policy, 1964–70', in R. Coopey, S. Fielding and N. Tiratsoo (eds), *The Wilson Governments, 1964–70*, Pinter, 1993.

HEATH AND BRITISH ENTRY, 1970–74

135 *Britain and the European Communities*, Cmnd 4715, HMSO, 1971.

136 Butler, David and Michael Pinto-Duschinsky, *The British General Election of 1970*, Macmillan, 1971.

137 Campbell, John, *Edward Heath: A Biography*, Jonathan Cape, 1993.

138 Kitzinger, Uwe, *Diplomacy and Persuasion: How Britain Joined the Common Market*, Thames and Hudson, 1973.

139 Lord, Christopher, 'Sovereign or confused? The great debate about British entry to the European Community twenty years on', *Journal of Common Market Studies*, 30/4, 1992.

140 Lord, Christopher, *British Entry to the EC Under the Heath Government of 1970–74*, Dartmouth, Aldershot, 1993.

141 Schenck, Catherine R., 'Britain and the Common Market', in Richard Coopey and Nicholas Woodward (eds), *Britain in the 1970s*, UCL Press, 1996.

142 Spanier, David, *Europe Our Europe*, Secker and Warburg, 1972.

143   Young, John W., 'The Heath government and British entry into the
      European Community', in Stuart Ball and Anthony Seldon (eds),
      The Heath Government, 1970–74, Longman, Harlow, 1996.
144   Young, Simon Z., *Terms of Entry: Britain's Negotiations with the
      European Community,* Northumberland Press, 1973.

THE LABOUR GOVERNMENTS, 1974–79

145   Benn, Tony, *Against the Tide: Diaries, 1973–76,* Hutchinson, 1989.
146   Butler, David and Uwe Kitzinger, *The 1975 Referendum,* 2nd edn,
      Macmillan, 1996.
147   Butler, David and Dennis Kavanagh, *The British General Election of
      February 1974,* Macmillan, 1974.
148   Callaghan, James, *Time and Chance,* Collins, 1987.
149   Castle, Barbara, *The Castle Diaries, 1974–76,* Weidenfeld and
      Nicolson, 1980.
150   Dell, Edmund, *A Hard Pounding: Politics and Economic Crisis,
      1974–76,* Oxford University Press, Oxford, 1991.
151   Healey, Denis, *The Time of My Life,* Penguin, Harmondsworth,
      1990.
152   Holmes, Martin, *The Labour Government 1974–79: Political Aims
      and Economic Reality,* Macmillan, 1985.
153   King, Anthony, *Britain says Yes: The 1975 Referendum on the
      Common Market,* American Enterprise Institute, Washington, DC,
      1977.
154   Ludlow, Peter, *The Making of the European Monetary System,*
      Butterworth, 1982.
155   Wilson, Harold, *Final Term: The Labour Government, 1974–76,*
      Michael Joseph, 1979.

THE THATCHER GOVERNMENTS, 1979–90

156   Allen, David, 'British foreign policy and west European cooperation',
      in Peter Byrd (ed.), *British Foreign Policy Under Thatcher,* Philip
      Allan, Oxford, 1988.
157   Burgess, Michael, *Federalism and European Union: Political Ideas,
      Influences and Strategies in the European Community, 1972–87,*
      Leicester University Press, Leicester, 1989.
158   Cockfield, Lord, *The European Union: Creating the Single Market,*
      Wiley, 1994.
159   Freedman, Lawrence, 'The case of Westland and the bias to Europe',
      International Affairs, 63/1, 1986.
160   Gamble, Andrew, *The Free Economy and the Strong State: the
      Politics of Thatcherism,* 2nd edn, Macmillan, 1994.
161   Howe, Sir Geoffrey, *Conflict of Loyalty,* Macmillan, 1994.

162 Kavanagh, D., *Thatcherism and British Politics: The End of Consensus?*, Clarendon Press, Oxford, 2nd edn, 1990.

163 Lawson, Nigel, *The View From No. 11*, Bantam Press, 1992.

164 Thatcher, Margaret, *The Downing Street Years*, Harper Collins, 1993.

165 Young, Hugo, *One of Us*, Macmillan, revised edn, 1993.

THE 1990s

166 Baker, David, Andrew Gamble and Steve Ludlam, 'The parliamentary siege of Maastricht 1993: Conservative divisions and British ratification', *Parliamentary Affairs*, 47/1, 1994.

167 *Draft Treaty of Amsterdam*, Coreper/European Commission, Brussels, 1997.

168 Duff, Andrew, Roy Pryce and John Pinder, *Maastricht and Beyond: Building the European Union*, Routledge, 1994.

169 George, Stephen and Ben Rosamond, 'The European Community', in Martin J. Smith and Joanna Spear (eds), *The Changing Labour Party*, Routledge, 1992.

170 George, Stephen, 'Britain and the IGC', in Geoffrey Edwards and Alfred Pijpers (eds), *The Politics of European Treaty Reform*, Pinter, 1997.

171 Jones, Tudor, *Remaking the Labour Party: From Gaitskell to Blair*, Routledge, 1996.

172 *Partnership of Nations: The British Approach to the European Union Intergovernmental Conference 1996*, HMSO, 1996.

173 Seldon, Anthony, *Major: A Political Life*, Weidenfeld, 1997.

INDEX